W9-BDT-094

Mending Wounded Minds

Beth Henry

With Vincent L. Pastore, Ph.D.

New Horizon Press
Far Hills, New Jersey

New Horizon Press
P.O. Box 669
Far Hills, NJ 07931

Beth Henry
  Mending Wounded Minds: Seeking Help for a Mentally Ill Child

Cover Design: Robert Aulicino
Interior Design: Susan M. Sanderson

Library of Congress Control Number: 2003105902

ISBN: 0-88282-242-X
New Horizon Press

Manufactured in Canada

2007   2006   2005   2004   2003   /   5   4   3   2   1

Table of Contents

Foreword

Vincent L. Pastore, Ph.D.

I first came in contact with the Henry family and their son Thomas through one of the therapists at the local mental health agency I worked for at the time. This particular therapist was a veteran of the Division of Social Services and the *Willie M.* program in North Carolina. I was impressed by how this seasoned therapist had been moved and concerned by this particular family as she worked the case in my office. We developed a game plan to assist the family as quickly as possible, assign a case manager and make application to the now-defunct *Willie M.* program, a program designed for the most disturbed and violent children in our state.

What I soon realized was, like every other complex client presentation, this was a case that would require a great deal of resources over a long period of time. What was different about this client was the fact that Beth was his stepmother. Once I met Beth, it was hard not to be swept up in her passion and commitment to do everything she could to assist her stepson, her family, her husband and her community. As an agency, we strive to provide every child in our services the same level of commitment to treatment. With Beth, we knew we had a parent who would both lead and be a part of our team in this quest.

Beth's approach to advocating for her stepson set her apart. I found her insight and zeal to be both refreshing and educative. Too often our society views children with mental disabilities as "parts," rather than as total human beings. Ms. Henry's description of positive advocacy reminds us not just about the "whole" child, but the interconnectivity of our culture in how we approach complex human emotions. What I have found extremely moving is how much love and empathy she exhibits during every step along her family's journey.

Over the past three years, there have been several important books written about how we are raising our male children. *Raising Cain*, by Kindlon and Thompson, and *Real Boys*, by William Pollack have helped us to see that when it comes to our sons, we fail miserably in giving them the language of emotions and a sense of being loved. Instead, all too often, they act from a place of shame and a sense of not being "good enough." What we don't do well is provide a "free and protected" space for our boys in an environment that provides safety and "holding."

Parents often struggle when it comes to their boys about how much love to give and until what age. They are afraid that their sons will not be tough enough and fail miserably as men. Unfortunately, this approach frequently dooms boys and men to lives of emotional struggle. In this book, Ms. Henry has answered these cultural questions on a very personal level, by saying there is never too much love to give to your sons or daughters, regardless of what they have done. It is a simple, yet eloquent, message: By understanding your child or your fellow human being, you are more apt to have compassion for him or her, and come from a place of empathy and love in your interactions with the individual.

And therein lies the secret of Ms. Henry's approach to life and advocacy. As advocates committed to any person or cause, we will experience many emotions. These emotions, especially anger, can be very useful in achieving our goals, especially when we realize that anger is nothing more than an energy. Turning this emotion into a positive energy to effect change is the ultimate goal for all of us. It fuels our passion and compassion and moves us to achieve what we did not believe attainable.

The benefits of this approach not only include improving the human condition, be it in general or one person at a time, but also being at peace with yourself and those around you. Ultimately, it helps not only those we care about, but it helps us as well. It helps us to stretch out and grow past the boundaries we believe to be unmovable in our own personality. Ms. Henry's story is a perfect example of how she has grown as a person while helping her stepson and her family.

As a parent or a mental health professional, you will find her story touching, full of courage and insight. She allows the story of her family to unfold slowly as she introduces us to a philosophy we have heard many times before: act with the same kindness, as you would expect to receive from others. In return, given this opportunity, those around us will want to find a way to do the right thing. Ms. Henry's story provides us with the knowledge of what it is like to be a parent of an emotionally disturbed child. It also provides us with the rare insight of what it is like to be that parent attempting to navigate the mental health and medical insurance companies systems of care.

With true Southern wisdom, Ms. Henry takes us step-by-step on this journey of becoming an advocate for those you love and care about who are mentally ill. She does not hit us over the head with it. Instead, she approaches this journey as she does every other journey in her life: with kindness, great care and a positive, yet tireless, energy. She identifies the major obstacles or stumbling blocks likely to face parents confronted with the multi-limbed, multi-systemic organism we call mental health services. She prescribes an approach in dealing with each of these obstacles within the system of positive advocacy she has developed. Then she breaks each one of these down to achievable and manageable steps. Through all of her advice runs the same theme: educate yourself, assert your needs with kindness and positive expectations, lead by example and let the team do its job.

While I was reading Beth's story, I couldn't help but have the feeling that something about her approach was not being captured in the written word. Finally, I realized that what Ms. Henry hints at, but doesn't spell out, are the intangible personal qualities needed: courage, honesty, good humor, good judgment, the willingness to press on, the willingness to be flexible, the desire to do good for the sake of others and the willingness to stretch out of one's comfort zone. These qualities are essential if positive advocacy is to work effectively.

To be sure, Ms. Henry and her family have been blessed with the presence of excellence when they most needed it. Her case manager was a passionate individual who went "above and beyond" for each of her clients. The manager and owner of the group home in which her stepson resides is one of the kindest gentlemen I have ever met. However, I have also noticed that Beth's willingness to live the qualities of positive advocacy is infectious and inspires those around her to reach higher and achieve the impossible. It is my wish for you, the reader, to be infected by this quality and pass it on. Pass it on to your spouse, your children, your fellow parents and the professionals involved in your mentally ill child's life.

—part one—

A Step Into Madness

Giggles of nervousness were coming from us, as we all piled into the judge's office. My twelve-year-old son Jeff was videotaping the ceremony, Kyle, his younger brother, provided encouragement; my ten year old daughter Jessica was taking photographs. She was dressed in the special white dress I'd bought her, wearing flower combs in her hair to match mine. At this moment, Mark and I and the children were becoming a real family. The world seemed to revolve around us as the judge began the ceremony. Tears welled up in our eyes when Mark and I recited our vows, meaning every single word we spoke to each other. A phone ringing on the judge's desk abruptly interrupted our mood. We just couldn't believe it when he actually took the call. Suddenly, we were thrust back into reality. We just stared at each other. You could tell Mark and I were thinking the same thought. *How could this happen at our wedding?* We gave each other a knowing smile. Mark gripped my hand a little tighter. The call seemed to take forever. As the judge hung up the phone, he looked up from his desk as if he'd suddenly remembered he was in the middle of a wedding ceremony and said, "You may kiss your bride, son." Our dream was restored. Mark's lips felt tender against mine as the moment I had awaited for so long was upon me. I had found the love of my life. No matter what, we would be together until death do us part. God had given me just what I prayed for, my soul mate. Now it was my turn to keep my promise to Him. I had found a man who loved me with all of his heart and treated me wonderfully. I was the luckiest woman on earth. I was so glad to be me.

Two of our friends who had wanted to witness our wedding had been unable to make it during their work day. Instead, Rick and Meghan asked us to dinner to celebrate. Our favorite restaurant was the Monterey Café, so we met them there that night. We enjoyed a festive dinner of Mexican food. The waiter served us a free dessert in honor of our marriage. As we said good night to our friends and walked to the car, we burst out laughing. The Toyota was decorated from top to bottom in shaving cream and balloons, just as if we were first time newlyweds. Rick was responsible, sneaking outside when he said he was going to the restroom. On the ride home in our gaily festooned car, we hoped people saw us; we wanted the whole world to know we were married and just how happy we were. Our wedding night was one of the most romantic nights of my life. Alone together as husband and wife, we held each other, not wanting to ever let go. Unfortunately, as every Navy wife quickly learns, duty soon called. Mark was due to leave in another twenty-four hours. We felt sad, but took comfort from the fact that this time he would be kissing his wife goodbye. He was really mine.

Shortly after we were married, Mark was transferred to shore duty in Virginia. We were so excited to be making a new start in a wonderful new place. I just knew we would love living near the beach. Virginia was to be the beginning of our new life together. We didn't know it then, but my promise to love Mark, for better or worse, would be sorely tested.

– c h a p t e r   o n e –

Virginia Here We Come

The drive to Virginia went as smoothly as a car trip can with three excited children packed into a cramped Toyota. We had decided to rent a three-bedroom townhouse that had plenty of space for our family. Mark and I moved into our home filled with the invincible feeling that nothing could ever hurt us. Our troubled first marriages were just episodes we both hoped to put far behind us as we started our new life together. Things just seemed to be going so right for us, giving us a sense of security. Mark was a Navy man and had occasional deployments at sea, but while he was gone, I kept myself busy.

Mark's new land-based job was exciting to him and it was a comfort to know that we wouldn't face any more time apart due to his assignments at sea. It didn't take me long to find a job as a veterinary receptionist. Our lives were settling into normalcy very quickly. Working, however, and being away from my children during the day wasn't something I wanted to do; it was something I had to do. Mark was paying $650 a month in child support for his sons Tommy and Bobby. For us this was a tremendous financial strain. Having me work full time to augment his salary was the only way to meet this obligation. Mark missed his children terribly. Many nights I heard him crying himself to sleep because of this void in his life. I wanted so much to be able to fill it for him. A man who loved and wanted his children with him so much was very special. Desperately, my heart wanted to ease his pain. Even though he seemed to be enjoying my children, devoting his free time to Jeff, Kyle and Jessica, I knew his heart was still aching for his boys.

That summer Mark's elder son, Tommy, had a tonsillectomy. Not being there when he had surgery made Mark worry about him all the more. Mark had always been an active father. He cooked the meals for his wife and the children, freezing them so that they would eat well when he was out to sea. When he was home on shore leave from the Navy, he took the boys on outings. He relished his time with them. Unfortunately, when left with their mother, the boys had been left in their cribs most of the day, or propped up with bottles in a beanbag chair in front of the television for hours at a time. Mark spent a lot of time trying to keep the boys quiet when he was home. Twice in Florida, each time during one of Mark's cruises, child protective services had been called because of Tommy's excessive screaming. When Social Services got in touch with Mark after his return, the matter was always dropped.

Bobby, Mark's younger son experienced mysterious seizures at birth. Because of this, Bobby had remained in the hospital for several days. Mark had tried to make it home at least every two weeks, so he could cook and clean the apartment and spend time with the boys. It was a long trip, but he loved his boys and wanted to be with them. Bobby had developed failure to thrive while a baby. It started when Mark's ship was dry-docked in South Carolina for several months. During that period both boys lived alone with their mother. Bobby had weighed a perfectly normal weight of sixteen pounds at six months old, but when Mark returned to active duty he had rapidly begun losing weight. By January, Bobby lost enough weight to alarm the doctors. Mark and his wife took Bobby for tests at Reno Children's Clinic in Jacksonville, Florida. They determined that he had failure to thrive. Some psychologists feel that this disorder occurs when an infant does not feel a loving bond with his mother and literally tries to starve himself to death. Deprivation of an emotional bond with a parent can create "learned helplessness" in babies, one that thwarts their drive to survive. These babies usually vomit in the presence of their mother. If anyone else fed Bobby, he would keep his formula and food down just fine; Bobby never threw up when his dad was taking care of him. When the parents told the specialist that they were moving because they were separating, Mark's wife was given the name of a specialist to follow up on Bobby's condition after the boys moved to Maine. Mark was providing the boys with insurance coverage through the military. Though Champus, the Navy's health care plan, would pay for the specialist in Maine, unfortunately, she never took Bobby to see the specialist. Bobby's emaciated appearance and the bald spots on his head were explained as the baby having a mysterious disease which kept him from gaining weight and growing hair. Family members accepted this explanation, although it did arouse their suspicions.

According to Mark, his wife's violent temper was painfully apparent. It was hard for others to believe, though. Gayle had the face of an angel and she portrayed herself as a victim though Mark said she confessed infidelities to him. Meanwhile, Mark, trying to save their marriage, suggested intense counseling. He tried as hard as he could to keep that family together, but he couldn't seem to make the marriage work.

Now we were struggling to pay Gayle child support each month. Though we both worked hard, we were broke before the end of the month. Finally, we decided we had to ask for a reduction in child support. Paying Gayle $650 a month, plus paying off the thousands of dollars of their marital debt, mostly Gayle's charges, which Mark had acquired in their divorce, was impossible to handle. The maximum child support amount in Maine for the children was actually $450 a month. Mark had told his lawyer that he would pay an extra hundred dollars a month in support, just to provide extra care for his children. The judge had made that an extra hundred, per child, per month. We were barely getting by each month and really needed a little of the financial pressure relieved. We placed a call to our lawyer in Maine. Not only was he respected professionally, but he was a heck of a nice guy. We suspected he reduced his rates and made things as simple and easy as he could for us because he knew we were financially strapped. We asked him to file a petition to reduce child support.

In September, Mark was no longer able to bear being apart from the boys. On the rare occasions Mark was allowed to speak to Tommy on the phone, the boy often seemed distant. Something inside Mark told him that the boys needed him. He was determined to make sure they were doing well, as their mother always reported, so Mark made a trip to his home state of Maine. Tommy and Bobby were both glad to see their dad. Mark's parents were delighted that he was home, but did voice concern over how the children were being cared for. Gayle had moved in with a man named Rod and was in her first trimester of pregnancy. They told him they felt Gayle's emotional instability was becoming apparent and the apartment was, in his parents' words, dirty and in disarray.

However, the most disturbing thing was the children's appearance. They were dressed in ragged clothing and both boys were very thin. Tommy seemed frightened and angry. Bobby was still acting like an infant at two years old, barely able to walk steadily.

Mark soon learned that Gayle's boyfriend Rod was unemployed, and Gayle was working to support him. He was barely twenty and good looking in a swarthy way. He spent most of his time babysitting Tommy and Bobby. Rod, we learned, seemed to make a habit of being alone with small children, and often volunteered to baby-sit them while their parents worked or partied. The whole situation made everyone, except Gayle, feel uneasy. Mark returned home with a whole new set of worries about his children.

Seeing Gayle pregnant made me realize that at thirty-two, my biological clock was ticking louder. A part of me wanted to have Mark's baby. However, our serious financial problems made that an impossible idea. In addition, Mark had had a vasectomy while he was married to Gayle. The Navy doctors would only tie, not cut, his vas deferens because of his young age. One day he experienced excruciating pain in his genital area. On a hunch, along with a physical examination, he had a sperm count done. The vasectomy had reversed itself. That had to be a sign from God that we were to have children together someday, I thought. How else could you explain such a wonderful twist of fate? Nevertheless, I felt jealous of his ex-wife. I wanted to be pregnant, but because of her, that was impossible.

While he was still in Maine, Mark spoke with me about his heartbreak after seeing the children. Then he called his lawyer, asking him to consider filing a petition for a custody change. We tried not to get our hopes up. I told him I would gladly support our taking care of the boys, but our assumption was that in Maine, a conservative state, no judge would ever give a father custody of his children. Mothers always prevailed in that state when it came to custody. A few weeks later our lawyer told us he had indeed filed the petition. As time passed, though, we began to get our hopes up that maybe, just maybe, it could happen. We could all be a real family.

Gayle didn't answer the custody petition. When it came time for the court hearing in February, the judge was furious with her because of her failure to respond. The judge had proof that Gayle had received the petition, adding further insult to the court. Along with a negative report from child services, the judge felt that Gayle's lack of interest in the case indicated that she didn't care and, in a hearing lasting only a few minutes, gave Mark custody of Tommy and Bobby. We felt that the judge couldn't have made a better decision. At that moment, in our eyes, he had become our hero.

― c h a p t e r   t w o ―

Becoming a Stepmother

Mark and I were joyful at the news that we had custody of the boys. Our minds were racing. Todd, our lawyer, told Mark that he had to get up to Maine fast to pick up Tommy and Bobby. We quickly made arrangements to do just that. The custody order arrived by overnight courier and Mark caught the next flight to Portland. His parents picked him up at the airport. Excitement filled the chilly night air as they drove to Mark's old hometown. Todd had advised Mark to take the police with him to acquire physical custody of the children since Todd wanted to take every precaution that there would be no trouble.

Accompanied by local police officers, Mark and his dad arrived at Gayle's apartment. The boys were watching from the window of their third floor apartment. Tommy began screaming for his father as soon as he saw him. Gayle yelled at Mark. However, in the end, she pretended to resign herself to the custody order, but begged to spend one more night with the boys. Mark agreed. The following morning he returned and picked up the boys. In the car he discovered the lunch their mother packed for them consisted of HoHos in a brown paper bag. In another grocery bag, she had packed a couple of tattered outfits that didn't even fit. None of their toys, not even a toothbrush, was given to Mark for the children.

That afternoon Mark, his dad, Tommy and Bobby began their long drive to Virginia. We had been advised that Mark should leave the state with the children as soon as possible, to prevent Gayle from trying to stop the court order.

I excitedly made plans for the boys' arrival. Jeff and Kyle made space in their room for their new stepbrothers. Kyle relocated to a futon downstairs. Jessica helped me clean the townhouse. We had already started the process of buying a new home. We would be moving soon. Unfortunately, the new home still only had three bedrooms. That didn't dampen our spirits. We happily made plans to convert the garage of the new house into a bedroom for Jeff and Kyle. Life seemed to be going our way. We were full of excitement and anticipation about our future.

Three A.M. was the anticipated time of the boys' arrival. I lay in bed sleepless while fantasies about our wonderful life with five kids, blended together by our love for each other, played over and over in my mind. Mark rang the doorbell around 3:45. Racing downstairs to stop the dogs from barking, I threw open the door. Before me stood Mark and his dad, holding two sleepy little boys. Bobby was placed in my arms. Instinctively, I flinched as I saw that he was as emaciated as the children on requests for aid for starving children in faraway refugee camps. His body was tiny and his head appeared unusually large and out of proportion. Bobby's limbs were so thin that you could see all of the bones in them. He seemed to have no muscle tissue at all. This child looked like a skin-covered skeleton. A roadmap of his veins could be easily seen through his tissue paper skin. Bald spots covered his head and his extremely thin hair was white from lack of pigment. As I held him, Bobby grunted, indicating discomfort. Tears came to my eyes. He was the most pathetic sight I had ever seen. Bobby was almost three.

Tommy didn't look much better. He also had thin skin, skinny limbs and visible veins all over his body. His ribs stuck out prominently, making his rib cage look huge in comparison to his body. His hair was dry and very brittle and also had spots without pigmentation.

Extremely notable was his very pointed head and slanted, widely set, eyes. When Mark's dad put him down, his movements were almost spastic. Dismissing my bristling instinct that something was seriously wrong, I carried Bobby upstairs. Mark followed with Tommy. When I changed Bobby's diaper (he still was not potty trained), I found a soft-ball-sized yeast infection on his right hip. We decided to put the boys in our bed for the night. The stairs were very close to the room they would be sleeping in. Mark and I were afraid that, because they were unfamiliar with the house, they might wander and fall.

We settled the boys in between us and an exhausted Mark soon dozed off. Sleep didn't come so easily to me. Nagging feelings that something was wrong kept me tossing and turning. This should have been a moment of blissful happiness. Why, I wondered, did I have the uneasy feeling that something was very wrong with these children? Was it just a case of new stepmother jitters? Was I critical of their appearance because they weren't my own? Over and over, I analyzed my thoughts. Despite the fact that I knew there was a natural enmity between me and the boys' mother, experience had taught me to always trust my instincts about my children and my instincts were on full alert that night. After a while, I settled on the rationalization that no matter what had been wrong in these boys lives, I was going to love them and fix it. Love was the one force I felt that I truly possessed and I just knew that love could cure anything and everything. I believed in its absolute power. That gave me confidence that I could help Tommy and Bobby. Finally, I fell asleep.

Startled by the alarm at six, we sleepily stumbled out of bed. The older kids had to get ready for school. However, the hustle and bustle of morning was soon interrupted by Tommy's shrill screams. He had gone downstairs to find our dog, B.J., eating the "lunch" that his mother had packed. Mark had inadvertently left the bag containing the HoHos in the dining room. Quickly scoping out unattended food, B.J. had found himself a forbidden chocolate treat. Tommy had tried to grab a HoHo from the dog for himself. In no uncertain terms, the dog had let Tommy know that the cakes were now his snack. B.J. was a gentle dog, but most animals are possessive with food. He had snapped at Tommy, scratching the boy's nose with his teeth. My heart pounded as I bounded down the steps, scooping Tommy into my arms. Mark was close behind. After we assessed the situation and found that despite the screams, there was not a crisis, we quickly calmed down. A Band-Aid and a kiss seemed to ease Tommy's upset. Mark's father Bob had decided to leave early that morning so that he could get back to Mark's mom, Perry. Her health was poor due to chronic asthma and emphysema, and he always stayed close by her side. Bob was a wonderful, caring husband. The love and concern he had for his wife made that very apparent. He fortunately had passed these wonderful qualities onto my husband.

Following Bob out to his car after we all ate a quick on-the-run breakfast, we said our emotional goodbyes. After he drove away, the realization that the boys were really staying with us hit me. It felt both joyous and scary. And the scary feeling was growing. Why on earth did I feel this way? I tried to shake off my uneasiness as we walked back inside the townhouse.

Both Mark and I had taken the day off from our jobs. After the older children left for school, we decided to take the boys shopping for some much needed new clothes and toys. Tommy and Bobby spent the entire drive pointing out every fast food sign we passed. Mark and I didn't know whether to be amazed at their intelligence or sad that they apparently had been deprived of home cooked meals. As an experienced mom, I realized I had to set up a routine for the boys. Mealtimes, bath time, bedtime, etc. would be at regular times every day. Fast food would be severely limited. I wanted to replace them with regular, home cooked, family meals. The first sit-down meal eaten was the lunch that I fixed that first day after we returned from our shopping trip. When asked what they would like to eat, Tommy replied, "ketchup and mustard sandwiches." The mere thought turned my stomach. When I set the wholesome food I'd prepared down on the table the boys grabbed for the food and wolfed it down while we watched, amazed and saddened by both their hunger and primitive eating habits.

Then we put them both on the sofa for a nap. Sleep deprivation from the night before was quickly catching up to Mark and me. The older children soon came home from school. We asked them to watch the boys. Mark and I went upstairs to our room to take a short nap. Not much time passed before we were startled awake by my daughter's screams. Jumping up, Mark and I ran downstairs. As we rounded the corner, Jessica cried out "Tommy tried to choke our cat. When I yelled at him he put his hands on his own neck and began choking himself."

Catching my breath, I tried to regain my composure, and blurted out, "Tommy, why on earth did you choke the cat?" Tommy was now standing before me with his hands tightly clasped around his own neck. His reply was one I will never forget. "That's how Rod choked me!" Mark and I just stared at each other with shocked expressions.

After what seemed like an eternal minute, Mark directed Jessica to put Tommy in the bed in her room for a nap. Then I turned to Mark. "Let's go upstairs. We need to talk."

Behind closed doors, Mark and I sat down on the bed, completely dumbfounded by what we had just witnessed. "Do you think Rod really choked Tommy?" he asked, shuddering.

I shook my head. "Look. I think we should spend the next couple of weeks making observations and let's not ask leading questions." I knew from reading about some of the trials of day care workers accused of child abuse that too much prodding could contaminate the memories in a child's mind. I wanted the children to tell us the truth. Mark and I decided to ask only simply "Why?" or "What happened?" questions when Tommy said or did something that concerned us. If Tommy disclosed something, we would merely say, "Thank you for telling me that" and make a conscious effort to show no emotion regarding the revelations. Believing the boys had been abused physically seemed unfathomable at the time. We knew they looked thin and neglected, but we had never even suspected physical abuse. After all, wouldn't someone in Maine have known about it before now?

By the day's end, Mark and I were bleary-eyed from exhaustion. The arrival of bath time seemed like a blessing. We told the boys to undress, planning to bathe them together. Bobby didn't seem to know what the word meant and I took his clothes off as you would an infant. Putting them in the tub, I noticed again how frail their little bodies were. They both looked truly pitiful. As the bath water began to fill the tub they both screamed with fear, clawing at me like frightened animals. Grabbing onto me in a death grip, they almost pulled me over into the tub with them. As we lifted the trembling children out of the water, Mark's and my eyes met. Each of us held one of them tightly; the children sobbed uncontrollably in our arms. Explaining to them that it was just a bath didn't seem to help. It took several minutes before they began to relax their grip and calm down. They were truly terrified.

"Dad," Tommy begged, "please, please." He pointed to the tub, and in the interests of calming their fears, Mark quickly undressed and got into the bath with them. I could tell Mark was uncomfortable, but he understood that they needed his reassurance that baths weren't going to harm them. Their bodies continued to tremble uncontrollably. Tommy hung on to Mark's neck for dear life. Bobby just stood in the water screaming. I hurried to wash them. We ended the bath as quickly as we could. We got them into their new nightclothes and they both began to settle down. Tucking them into bed, Mark and I stood there a while looking at them. "I'm just glad to be with them again," he whispered. I rejoiced with him that he had been reunited with his sons.

However, back in our room, Mark expressed his concern about the boys' behavior in the tub. "Tommy has always been like a fish when it comes to water. He loved it. When my dad and mom visited us in Florida, dad and I took Tommy swimming several times. Now he is totally afraid of water. It just doesn't make any sense."

I had been told that the two boys I was getting as stepchildren were extremely intelligent and really cute. The grandparents and Mark couldn't possibly have been talking about the two children now sleeping soundly in the next room. These children didn't resemble any normal two and four-year-olds I had ever seen before. Bobby acted like an infant. He would be turning three in two months time. Tommy seemed very slow compared to most four-year-olds. His verbal skills appeared limited and the scene with the cat was horrifying. Moreover, the children were more than thin, they were emaciated and tiny. My instincts were bristling. Thoughts churned in my mind all night. What was wrong with these kids? Was I just being judgmental or maybe just fearful, because they were the children of another woman? Was there more to this than met the eye? After several hours of lost sleep, I finally decided that the first thing to do was check them out physically.

Early the next morning I made an appointment to take the boys to the doctor at the Navy base for a physical. Their appearance was really disturbing to me, as my own children had never looked anything like they did. In the doctor's office Bobby was weighed first. He was only twenty-three pounds. He was wearing his clothes, including a jacket, at the time. That meant he actually weighed even less than that. Most one-year-olds weighed as much as he did. The doctor came in and I proceeded to explain the situation and my concerns. He checked the boys over carefully and prescribed medication for the yeast infection on Bobby's hip. That was it. He seemed oblivious that anything else could be wrong with them. Shock at Bobby's weight and appearance was overriding my ability to think of anything else. Navy doctors sometime aren't as concerned as they should be about medical problems and this physician was no exception. Still feeling uneasy, I resolved that I would take them over to the Navy satellite clinic and have them examined again. The nagging feeling, that something was very wrong, just wouldn't go away. Even if I looked like a fool, I was going to pursue my gut instincts.

The weekend seemed to sneak up on us quickly. Tommy and Bobby continued to scream and carry on over the slightest thing, a door closed too loudly, a new food. Despite all our attempts to show them love, those first days were pretty overwhelming. Mark and I decided to go out alone together for lunch on Saturday afternoon, so that we could reconnect and talk quietly with each other. Jeff, Kyle and Jessica agreed to baby-sit. They had always demonstrated a good sense of responsibility so I knew Tommy and Bobby were in capable hands. Lunch gave us a chance to be alone for the first time in several hectic days. Tommy and Bobby were the sole topics of conversation. Our concerns were plaguing both of us and we needed to figure out how to handle things. By the time we returned home, our mood was positive. We would do whatever it took to settle the boys into our family.

But the older children met us at the door with somber looks on their faces. "Tommy's been screaming since you left. We did everything we could to calm him down but he was having a fit and wouldn't stop cursing." They were so upset by his awful behavior that they had used the tape recorder on the answering machine to record some of his tirade. Reassuring the older kids that they had done everything right, we decided to introduce Tommy to the concept of a time-out. Maybe this would work. I believe consistency is the key with any discipline and we were determined to be 100 percent consistent with Tommy and Bobby so they would not only learn some rules of good behavior, but feel secure.

Mark had been letting the boys talk on the phone with their mother nightly at our expense. We felt it was the compassionate thing to do, since she must be missing them and they were separated from their mother. That afternoon, we got a call from Gayle's mother, Alice. I felt that it was important for the children to maintain ties with both sets of grandparents and her calling them was not a problem for me. I was, however, scared to death of talking to her. I had been told that she was a force to be reckoned with. Alice was a legend in her hometown. Everyone said she was a woman who you never wanted to make angry. Her reputation was intimidating to me. I had assumed that because I was now married to her ex-son-in-law, she would automatically feel animosity, if not hatred, for me. Hearing her voice on the other end of the line made me realize that I couldn't have been more wrong. Her friendly manner immediately put my perceived fears at ease. I actually found myself enjoying the conversation, telling her all about how the boys were doing. Tommy spoke to her on the phone, and much to my surprise, asked her if it was okay to call me "Mom." She reassured him that it was. At that moment, I realized that I was going to really like this woman, even if liking your husband's ex-mother-in-law did seem a little weird.

After hanging up the phone, Mark and I sat down on the sofa as the children played with some toys on the floor. Bobby was running in circles around the room. I had begun to notice that he seemed to do this a lot. Tommy approached me, and for the first time called me Mom. Mark had introduced me to him as Beth. While I was touched by the gesture, it also raised some concerns. Alone in bed that night, I asked Mark if he realized that over the past couple of days, neither child had cried out for their real mother. He had.

chapter three

Hopes and Nightmares

Still feeling uneasy about the boys appearance and behavior, I made an appointment with the clinic. Mark had to work, so I took the boys. The pediatrician, Amy Gordon, was a middle-aged graying woman who, unlike the first doctor to whom I'd taken Tommy and Bobby, did a more detailed examination. During the exam, I asked the doctor why Bobby had bald spots on his head. She looked at me matter-of-factly and said, "Malnutrition."

Dr. Gordon instructed me to get Tommy's shot records from his mother and, if I couldn't, to bring him back in a month for shots. I told her I would. My heart seemed to weigh a ton, under the strain of telling Mark that the doctor had diagnosed Bobby with severe malnutrition. He was as shocked as I had been. I could feel the depth of his pain and frustration when I told him the diagnosis.

Tommy frequently had tantrums and continued to claim that Rod had choked him. Bath time was still plagued by the screaming fits of the two frightened children. Our concerns were growing by leaps and bounds. After two weeks of this, Mark finally asked Gayle one evening on the phone if Rod had ever played really rough with the kids. She said no, but that they had been allowed to watch a popular police television show. This show featured real people being arrested by the police, sometimes resisting their arrest. Although Tommy's odd behavior did not seem to have anything to do with this kind of television show, her odd response raised a red flag. Gayle told Mark, during that conversation, that she knew the kids were better off with us. The March child support check had automatically been sent to Gayle by the military and Mark requested its return because we needed the money for the children. We also told her that we needed their immunization records and birth certificates. Without immunization records, Tommy was going to have to go through his entire childhood shot series again. Mark made it clear that ignoring our request would cause Tommy to suffer unnecessarily. She agreed to send everything the next day.

Contacting the mental health contractor for the military, we got permission to have Tommy and Bobby start seeing a therapist. Our concerns about what they may have been through were growing. We weren't sure what had happened to them, but we knew we had to find out. We had to get to the bottom of their strange behavior. Within two weeks of their arrival, they were seeing a licensed clinical social worker named Robin Jones. They immediately took a liking to Robin.

The immunization records and birth certificates never arrived. When Tommy's doctor's appointment rolled around, he had to get his shots all over again. Holding him down for his injections made me feel very angry with Gayle. He screamed horribly as the needle pierced his upper thigh. How could she have done this to a little kid? Why did I have to be the heavy and make him get the shots he probably didn't even need? My anger must have been apparent, judging by the look on Mark's face that night when he walked in the door. He shared my feelings emphatically. Gayle called that night and for the first time, he verbally lit into his neglectful ex-wife. Mark told her how irresponsible it was not to send the records. He told her how Tommy had fought and screamed while getting his shots. This was the first time I had ever seen Mark lose his temper with his ex-wife. I listened on the extension as in his upset state he blurted out that Tommy was saying that Rod had choked him. Gayle calmly stated that nothing like that had ever happened. She didn't ask any more questions and didn't even seem curious or concerned that her son was saying such things about a man she had only known a few months, and who'd been living with the children. She again promised to mail the child support check and the records. This time we didn't hold our breath. Two weeks later, it finally showed up. Better late than never, I guess.

Gayle's reassurance that she knew the boys were better off with us turned out to be untrue. The whole time, she had been having her neighbors write letters to the judge who had heard the original case, asking him to reconsider. Having learned of our our suspicions of abuse, she escalated her pleas to the judge that she was an innocent victim. The paperwork showed up on an afternoon I had off from work. My head started to spin as I read that the judge would be holding a new hearing for custody. Apparently, he felt he had acted in haste or anger, based on the impassioned letters from Gayle's friends and neighbors, and had made the wrong decision to take two small children away from their mother. Trembling, I dialed Mark at work. Racked with sobs, I told him about the new hearing. No date had been set. Mark's parents were as upset as we were when we told them about the new hearing. They were extremely supportive as they tried to offer us hope and words of comfort. That night, we finally told Mark's parents of our suspicions of abuse. They took it hard, but we felt they needed to know.

Shortly after we got the legal papers, Gayle and Rod were married. I strongly suspected that the old rule that a wife doesn't have to testify against her husband in a court of law played a big factor in their decision to marry.

Meanwhile, we were getting ready to move to our new house in a nearby neighborhood. The joy over our first home was dampened by the impending custody battle. Our dream was finally coming true and yet we were slipping into a nightmare.

Mark's parents came down to help us move. For a brief period, our joy at finally having a home of our own made us forget the impending legal battle with Gayle. Perry's health condition had worsened, but her delight at seeing her precious grandchildren again seemed to perk her up, making her feel better.

Our new home was small, but to us it seemed like a palace. The carpets were brand-new and the prettiest shade of soft mint green. We had a lovely fenced yard for the children to play in and our two dogs, B.J. and Buffy, had plenty of room to run.

The house was all on one level. It was pure heaven, not having to climb stairs all day long or to worry about Bobby navigating them. The great room was enormous and homey. Along the front wall was a wood stove, giving the house a cozy rustic feeling. The bedrooms were good sized. All four boys would share a large room with bunk beds and a futon. Jessica would have a room to herself. Our bedroom had a door that led to the backyard so we could watch the children. We felt like we were in heaven on moving day. It was ours, all ours. It should have been one of the happiest days of our lives, but an undercurrent of worry hung in the air. With the percussion of a judge's gavel against the bench, our newly blended family could be forever torn apart. By now, I had grown to love Bobby and Tommy. The fact that they needed so much love and care just made me want to be a mother to them that much more. They needed me and I was determined to keep them safe from further harm. They deserved a good life, especially after all that they had been through.

I quit my job just before we closed on the new house, so that I could devote all my time to the children and especially to Bobby and Tommy, whose need of a stay-at-home mother had become apparent in the preceding weeks. I knew Mark would feel better if I was at home with them all day. I spent a good part of my days quietly observing Tommy and Bobby, trying over and over to figure out just what was wrong with them. I felt like a detective, always searching for clues.

Bobby wanted to be held constantly and carried everywhere. He seemed absolutely clueless and even terrified when it came to potty training. The tiny child flapped his arms a lot, often holding them drawn up into a raised position in front of him. He often ran ritualistically in circles for minutes at a time, several times a day. I wondered who he might be running from. The most puzzling thing about him was his apparent inability to recognize his own personal needs. Bobby never said he was hungry, tired or even that he had messed in his pants. When we asked if he had soiled his pants, he would just tilt his head to the side, seeming not to understand. He often was very passive and had an extremely gentle nature. He reminded me of a new-born baby deer, so delicate and frail, easily frightened of the most innocuous stimuli. Loud noises made him cover his face with his tiny hands and begin crying, but most of the time he would just stare at you with a vacant look in his eyes. Sometimes, I found myself wondering if Bobby was really there at all.

However, it was Tommy who was beginning to seriously concern me. His movements were spastic and sometimes he twitched as he walked. He was unable or unwilling to answer simple questions coherently. For instance, when I asked him if he wanted a peanut butter sandwich for lunch, he would reply "dog bad." His replies made no sense. Other times, he seemed to be in another world completely. I made an appointment for him with the local Navy neurological specialist. Answers, I needed answers!

This time we sat down and gave the neurologist a complete history, which included our suspicions of abuse. She listened patiently. Then she requested that we take Tommy into the adjacent exam room, instructing us to undress him down to his underwear and put him on the examining table. He seemed unresponsive, sitting there almost detached, his face expressionless as she began examining him. The specialist then requested that we lay him down on the examining table. As Mark tried laying him down, Tommy began to struggle forcefully! The doctor proceeded with her examination, hooking her forefinger under the band of Tommy's underwear to lower it and examine his genitals. As he felt his underwear being lowered, Tommy screamed, "Oh no! *Oh no!*" at the top of his lungs. Mark and I stared at each other. Dear God, was it even possible that the abuse had been sexual too? The doctor made her genital exam brief as Tommy fought her probing. Afterward, I picked up a trembling, visibly shaken, Tommy in my arms. I held him as tightly as I could. "It's all right," I said over and over trying my best to comfort him. The doctor said that she hadn't seen anything neurologically significant, but that she would do blood tests at an appointment next week. She would test him for high lead levels, since he had been living in an older apartment with his mother. Circumstances indicated that the children might have come in contact with lead-based paint. Still reeling from Tommy's eerie screams, we left her office and began driving home.

Mark and I didn't talk much on the way. We both knew what the other was thinking. How bad was this going to get? What had been done to these children?

Gayle's mother kept in touch regularly. A bond was forming between us because of our love for the children. I considered telling her of our suspicions of abuse, but I was hesitant. This was her daughter and new son-in-law that I was accusing. When Alice and Gayle's dad, Will, decided they would visit us, I knew I would have my chance to talk to them at that time and could make up my mind then how much to say. Tommy was now telling us that Rod had held him under the bath water, trying to drown him. Haltingly, he also told us bits of stories of how Rod had held Bobby upside down in the toilet. Though Tommy's vocabulary was scanty, his memories always remained consistent regarding the abuse. He said Rod did it because Bobby had made a mess in his pants. Now we understood why Bobby screamed and screamed when we tried to get him to sit on the toilet. Meanwhile, Tommy, to our horror, had begun smearing feces on the walls. His bedroom and our bathroom walls often displayed his foul-smelling fecal artwork. He would actually dig into his rectum with his fingers to provide himself with the "paint." I remembered reading that fecal smearing was one of the most obvious signs that a child was seriously disturbed. These children had obviously been through something very severe. I needed to know what the grandparents had observed. I decided to tell them of our suspicions when they visited. Anxiety was coursing through me as I rehearsed my words over and over in my mind. How would they take these serious accusations? Would they even believe me?

Will and Alice called us as soon as they arrived in town. We drove over to the motel where they were staying to meet them. The moment I laid eyes on them I knew that they were people that I would not only like, but love. Alice had the sweetest face, with a magnetic smile that revealed her softhearted soul. Her laugh was totally musical, her warmth radiated around her like a beautifully glowing aura.

Will was a ruggedly handsome, tall, very muscular man with an irresistible smile that made you smile back. Will kept the children and me laughing with his humor. When you were with him, you just felt good; you couldn't help yourself. As a young father, he and Alice had survived his bout with cancer. But Will was a lot like the Energizer Bunny. He just kept on going and going and going. A part of me fell in love with him that day. His obvious sensitivity and concern for his family were heartwarming. I knew that Alice and Will both had a strong sense of morality and family. I could see they would be a part of my family, bound to me by their grandchildren. I felt privileged to be a part of their lives. If loving Tommy and Bobby had taught me one thing, it was that family really has nothing to do with blood and genes. How much you love someone is what really makes the person family.

When we sat down to talk, I could feel my pulse throbbing uncomfortably in my neck as I started to tell them about our problems with the boys. They listened as I spoke, tears welling up in their eyes. The instant I told them about the boys' scene with the bath water, Alice responded that she thought what Tommy was telling us had to be true. Then she told us of an incident that had happened the previous summer. Gayle had been away for a weekend, and Rod was left alone to baby-sit the boys. Alice had the boys stay over at her house the following week. "Tommy always loved bath time. That child would have spent forever in the tub if you let him," she said wistfully. "Only now, something was very different and very wrong." When Alice put on the water, Tommy had started screaming, "Shut off, *shut off!*" and threw a tantrum until she did, climbing over Alice to escape the bathtub. Later, I found out Tommy's bizarre behavior that day had embedded itself vividly in her mind. That incident echoed our own observations and was the key we needed to begin to unlock the truth. We felt Tommy was very brave to have told us about what he had experienced and now we needed to find out more. Our conversation with his grandparents was just the reinforcement we needed to protect the boys. Will and Alice said they would support our petition to keep custody. Knowing they were going to help us was such a comfort. Alice told me her gut instinct was that the boys would be much better off with us. One thing I would learn about Alice, in time, was that her instincts were always dead on. In fact she helped me by telling me to listen to my gut. "It always knows the right thing to do," she said.

Tommy and Bobby loved seeing their grandparents again. Alice and

Will told me over and over how good the boys were looking and I felt the same way. Bobby was getting the first new growth of hair in his bald spots and his roots were now showing dark brown pigment. Dark hair, like his father's, was beginning to take the place of the white patches of hair on Bobby's head, which we had learned were a sign of the malnutrition he had suffered. Both boys had gained some weight and their skin was no longer dry and itchy, nor did their veins prominently show through. Tommy even told his nana proudly, "I get three meals a day and snacks, too." Coming from a regular kid this wouldn't mean much, but coming from a child whose ribs had stuck out so far you could count them, it meant the world. In addition to nourishing food, Bobby was on a special high calorie shake that I had invented. The shake consisted of milk, Carnation Instant Breakfast, and Carnation Sweetened Condensed Milk. He was thriving on it. His body even seemed to be gaining some proportion in relation to his head size. I felt that my hard work and stabilizing routines were paying off.

On the last day of the boys' grandparents' visit, we went to Denny's Restaurant for breakfast. Later, Alice told me that this was the first pleasant meal in a restaurant that she had ever had with Tommy. Before he came to live with us, she said, "I always had to interrupt our meal and take him outside because of his tantrums." Knowing that she thought I was doing a good job meant a great deal to me. I wasn't going to let her down. I was committed to doing all I could to help these two little boys.

Saying goodbye was hard when it came time for Alice and Will to leave. Jeff, Kyle and Jessica already thought of them as grandparents and were so sad when they left. Mark said he had seen a completely new side of his ex-in-laws. His relationship with them was now so much stronger than it had been when he was married to Gayle. When he'd been married to their daughter, Mark had been told that Alice didn't like him. Their visit to Virginia had not only improved the relationship, it had drawn them very close.

Alice and I joked that our new relationship was so unusual it could be the focus of a talk show episode.

Mark, the kids and I couldn't wait till their next visit. We had so much fun being together, even though the heartbreak over Tommy and Bobby lingered in the air. Unfortunately, we soon found their visit had created more fear in Tommy. He managed to communicate that he had been afraid they would take him back to Maine after their visit. We all had to constantly reassure him that he was going to stay with us. Even so, his unruly behavior accelerated, as did his uncontrollable crying episodes. Watching him I kept asking myself what else was locked up inside this child's mind? I was so afraid we were going to find out that it was something even more horrible than what we had learned.

I reported what Alice had told me to Tommy's counselor. Slowly but surely, the troubled child was starting to reveal the abuse he had suffered to her. With her added advice giving me reassurance, I kept up the routines I had established, making sure that I was always consistent in everything I said and did when it came to the boys. They needed the rigid structure. These kids needed to know that they could always trust me to tell them the truth. I always told Tommy and Bobby that I would never lie to them about anything and I never have. They needed to be able to trust the people caring for them completely. Nevertheless, Bobby was slow to progress emotionally. He did not make the visible progress of a normal child. Attempts to potty train him were failures, but considering his memories, I didn't push the issue. Just taking him into the bathroom often caused him to begin crying and screaming in terror. Each time I held him close to my heart, stroking his hair to calm him, I could get him to sit on the toilet. Even so, the tiny little boy firmly latched his spindly arms around my neck, seeming to hold on for dear life. It was heartbreaking to see him suffering this way. Potty training should have been a great time of self-confidence building. Instead, for Bobby it was a reminder of something terrifying in his past.

Tommy was getting progressively worse with each passing week. I tried hard to love his horrific pain out of him, but the trauma was just too strong. He was having full-blown attacks of what I later learned was Post-Traumatic Stress Disorder (PTSD). This is a syndrome that often affects victims of severe trauma. The sufferer can actually relive the trauma, in his or her mind mind, through flashbacks. During a flashback, the victim actually feels the sensation, as if they were reliving the traumatizing situation all over again. When he had an attack of PTSD, Tommy's eyes glazed over as if he could only see the past, not the present or the people standing helplessly in front of him. His world was one of terror. Before him stood love, caring and hope, but his painful withdrawal into the past blinded him to it. Without warning, he would begin screaming at us pointing, yelling and accusing us of calling him the foulest of curse words when all we'd expressed were loving sentiments. He would back himself up against the wall, flailing himself wildly against it, as if trying to escape a horror of mammoth proportion. As the attacks wound down, he would crouch into a fetal position on the floor and become very still. These episodes made us all feel so helpless. There seemed to be nothing any of us could do to reassure him of our love, but we tried everything we could think of, hoping we could break through the wall between him and us. Eventually, we learned to just stand there until the attack was over, which was sometimes over an hour after it had started. Meanwhile, his shrieks of sheer terror frightened us, even though we all knew what was going on and understood by that time the trauma he was suffering. Nevertheless, when he started screaming, the children would run around the house, making sure all the windows were shut. We all felt terrified that the neighbors, oblivious to Tommy's emotional problems, would think that we were hurting the boy. At night, when all was quiet, I could still hear his shrieking screams in my exhausted mind. Over and over, I prayed to the Lord to help me find a way to help these wounded children heal.

However, as time passed more bizarre and upsetting behavior began to emerge. Early one morning, as Kyle was sleeping, Tommy got out of his bed and stood beside Kyle's. Then he proceeded to urinate all over the foot of the bed. When we found out what had happened, we were totally shocked, and hoped it was a one-time thing. Of course, it wasn't. Tommy began regularly urinating all over Bobby as he slept. Bobby never said a word. He would lie there and let Tommy urinate all over him. The next morning, Bobby would get up and not even try to communicate about his soaked bed and clothing. However, the stench of Tommy's urine quickly brought Bobby's humiliation at the hands of his older brother to our attention. We couldn't get Tommy to stop. We tried talking to him, pleading with him, having him clean up his mess himself, time-out and even spanking as a last resort. Absolutely nothing worked. Every morning,the bedroom, as well as Bobby, smelled sickening.

We asked ourselves what we were supposed to do. Even Tommy's therapist was unable to help us stop his bizarre behavior. Naturally, the older boys couldn't stand the smell in the room and we moved Tommy into his own room, the room that had belonged to Jessica. Jessica had to share the room with Bobby. Jeff and Kyle moved into the living room. It really upset me that Jessica, Jeff and Kyle had to give up their rooms, but we didn't know what else to do.

As I lay awake night after night I wondered how the judge in Maine could even consider returning these children to the hell from which we'd taken them. Sleep just wouldn't come. I prayed to God for help, replaying everything over and over in my mind. In the silence of the darkness, I continually figured out creative new ways to try to help Tommy and Bobby. However, in the light of day nothing I tried worked. Nevertheless, I refused to give up. I did have success in getting Tommy enrolled in special education preschool. I hoped this would at least address his developmental delays.

Gayle gave birth to a daughter shortly after Alice and Will went back home. Alice was there for the birth and so was Rod. We all feared for the baby's safety at the hands of her father and mother. I found myself very depressed over her birth. Meanwhile, my own yearning for a child with Mark had been growing every day. Mark and I had stopped using birth control; we had decided that we wanted a child together, a symbol that despite all we were going through our love and family would persevere and flower.

chapter four

Moments of Joy, Days of Pain

Whenever Gayle called Tommy, his tantrums noticeably escalated for days afterward. The calls were a recurring nightmare that we all dreaded. Each time the phone rang, my heart began to beat wildly in my chest, wondering if it was Gayle. I was scared to answer it and scared not to. Just about the time we managed to stabilize things in the aftermath of the last call, she called again and upset him. Desperate to know what she was saying that was triggering his upset, we bought a speakerphone so we could begin monitoring the calls. It didn't take long after we started putting the calls on speaker to figure out why he got so upset after talking to her. Tommy had apparently been telling his mother about the abuse perpetrated on him by Rod. We discovered that Gayle insisted to Tommy that nothing had ever happened to him, that Rod had never hurt him. We were furious, knowing his mother's denial was probably the worst possible psychological damage being inflicted on Tommy.

Meanwhile our life was becoming increasingly tense. As Tommy acted out more and more, much of my day was spent trying to convince him that his daddy and I loved and believed him and trying to calm him through his stress attacks. In fact, I was so involved with Tommy's problems that I didn't even notice that I was a week late for my menstrual period.

When I realized this I made an appointment at Navcare for a pregnancy test. The test came back negative. That made me feel totally foolish. They told me to come back in two weeks if I still hadn't started my period. For the next two weeks nausea consumed me every morning. Either I had to be pregnant or I was losing my mind. My stress level was, after all, definitely at an all-time high. Chronic sleep deprivation had me even wondering if I was imagining my complaints.

One morning we took Tommy and Bobby to the shopping center nearby for a change of pace. It turned out to be a good idea until Mark began backing the Toyota out the space where we'd parked. At that moment a full sized van that had been stopped several feet behind us, started backing up very quickly. Apparently, the driver was backing up so that he could let someone out of a parking space that he wanted. Mark saw the man's van coming towards our car and blew the horn. It was too late. The next thing we felt was impact!

After making sure the kids and I were okay, Mark went to talk to the other driver. My heart sinking at the thought of further bills, I got out of the car and inspected the damage. The entire trunk of our car was pushed in and the tail light was damaged. A few minutes later Mark came back to talk to me. He had called the town police, but they said that they didn't respond to accidents in private parking lots. We exchanged insurance information with the guy, who was also a sailor.

As we drove home, I couldn't stop my tears. We just didn't need more trouble. Mark called the guy that hit us. Both men agreed to fix their own damage.

After two weeks passed I was feeling too embarrassed to go back to *Navcare*. I went to the store and bought a home pregnancy test. I didn't have too much faith in them, but I figured another possible embarrassment at the doctor's office made it worth trying a home test. After I did the test, a faint purple line appeared. I grabbed the box. Over and over, I reread the part about how even a faint line meant pregnancy. When I called Mark at work and told him the results, Mark was delighted but, like me, distrusted home tests. "Better go back to the clinic," he suggested, "before we celebrate."

That afternoon, I went to the Naval Base clinic for a pregnancy confirmation. They did a urine test, again done with afternoon urine. In early pregnancy, sometimes only morning urine will have enough HCG hormones in it to indicate pregnancy on professional tests. The test was negative. I burst out crying, telling the doctor that I had been pregnant with three other children and that I knew why I was throwing up every morning. To pacify me, he sent me to the laboratory for a blood test. Blood tests for HCG are more sensitive. They can confirm pregnancy earlier. They said it would take an hour. Nervous, I sat down to wait.

The guy from the laboratory came to the desk in about ten minutes and kept grinning at me while he talked to the nurse. I finally asked the grinning corpsman if my blood test was back early. He explained that, although delayed, the urine test had turned positive and that the blood test had just confirmed the urine test's results. I was definitely pregnant.

Driving home was a total blur. Somehow, I seemed to be pulling into my driveway before I even knew I was there. I raced into the house and grabbed Mark. "We're definitely pregnant." Our spirits were lifted as we called his parents, my parents, and Will and Alice. Everyone was overjoyed. We all desperately needed something good to happen to lift our dejected spirits. Unfortunately, our happiness was short lived. Not even a week later I miscarried twins.

The next few days were a blur. I was so out of it that when I went to the bank, I left the money I had just withdrawn on the counter and walked to my car. The kind teller had immediately taken the money I left and put it in a safe place. She gave me a big smile as I walked back into the bank. She handed me the money and I thanked her. But my depression over losing our babies was enormous. I was just going through the motions, trying to get through the hours and take care of Bobby and Tommy whose tantrums were ongoing. To give us some private time to grieve, we turned off our phones for a few days.

Meanwhile, Tommy had begun revealing terrible things to us that indicated that he and Bobby might have been sexually abused. Tommy's newest revelations about the abuse explained a lot of his bizarre behaviors. As he disclosed more truly horrifying information, his PTSD attacks escalated. Tommy was telling us that Rod had locked him, Bobby and the other child he babysat in a closet naked together. I winced as it became apparent why he wanted to watch children all day.

Tommy gave us vivid descriptions of Rod wearing monstrous Halloween masks and coming into Tommy and Bobby's room to frighten them when they were asleep. He told us that Rod liked to stick his finger deep into Tommy's rectum. Tearfully, Tommy described Rod pulling out fecal matter from his behind during the assault. Tommy said Rod liked to show it to him. He said that Rod liked to pee in his mouth and all over him and Bobby. As we listened horrified, Tommy described Rod sticking his penis into his mouth and making Tommy suck on it. He clearly described the substance that came out of Rod's penis, although he called it "pee." The "pee" was "white," according to Tommy. White penile ejaculation wasn't something a normal four year old would even know about. Neither was anal penetration. Rod told Tommy if he didn't keep their "secret," he would kill them.

I was reeling from coping with the boys, the newest revelations and my grief over losing the twins. As soon as we turned the phones on, we got a phone call from our lawyer. He had just gotten a letter from Gayle's attorney. Gayle had told her lawyer that she had called the house and that the kids had been left alone in the tub while Mark and I were out having a good time. Through tears, I explained everything that had taken place in the past few days to our attorney. He apologized for having to disturb me with this problem, and called Gayle's lawyer and explained why we had been out of contact. The matter was dropped.

Realizing that I needed some help, I made an appointment to see a psychiatrist, Dr. Byers. Mark drove me to his office. Almost as soon as I sat down, I began pouring out the sadness of my miscarriage, the whole Tommy and Bobby saga, and ended with the latest letter from Gayle's attorney. Dr. Byers listened patiently. When I was finally talked out, he simply stated, "You're not crazy, you're just overwhelmed."

I had to smile at his statement. "Overwhelmed is quite an understatement," I said, but I felt better having talked to him.

Mark had a surprise waiting for me in the car. On the backseat

floor was a little milk-chocolate colored puppy. We named him
Wayne. The cute puppy took my mind off the miscarriage. Curiously,
Wayne was born the same day I lost the twins. The odd coincidence
made me feel that he was truly meant to be mine. I was beginning to
smile again. Mark's love never let me down.

In the days that followed we had to ready ourselves for the
upcoming custody hearing. Another call from our lawyer brought
further bad news. Gayle was claiming she had a conversation with
him before the original custody hearing. This would have been a serious breach of legal protocol. Even though his phone records showed
no such thing, our attorney felt he should recuse himself from the
case.

I pleaded with Todd not to give in. Hanging up the phone, I lay
my head on the kitchen table and sobbed for a good half-hour before
regaining my composure.

My head was spinning as I called Mark and told him what Todd
had said. Panicked, I called Mark's parents. Within a week, Mark's
dad had hired Burton Warner, a high-powered lawyer, to represent us.
Knowing we were almost broke by now from the bills, his dad said he
was going to pay for the lawyer to represent Mark and the boys. Will
and Alice had also gone to meet Mr. Warner. A strong bond was forming between those four special people in our lives. During Mark's
marriage to Gayle, the two sets of grandparents had been acquain-
tances, but the bond they now shared, fighting for their grandchildren's future together, had brought them close together.

Mark and I talked a lot about losing our babies. We decided that I
would make my six-week follow-up appointment with a nearby
physician. I just couldn't bear to go back to the Navy hospital. I
searched the phone book and found a woman gynecologist who was
less than a half-mile from our house. A Navy doctor had previously
told me that my uterus was prolapsed and I needed a hysterectomy. I
worried that maybe I couldn't carry a child full term due to this condition.

When I entered Dr. Ames' office, I could tell immediately that I liked
her. Mark and I took a seat in her office. Tears welling up in my eyes, I
began pouring out how I felt I couldn't carry a baby because of the prolapsed uterus. When I had finished, she began to smile. She told me I

was most likely wrong, that an exam would probably reveal otherwise. Mark and I looked at each other for confirmation that we were hearing her correctly. We then went to the exam room, where she had her nurse take some blood to run tests for possible thyroid problems. While she was doing the Pap smear, she suddenly pushed herself back from the table and started grinning at us. Puzzled looks crossed our faces. She asked us if we really wanted a baby. After what seemed like several minutes staring into Mark's face, I quietly answered yes. Mark echoed my answer. Dr. Ames told us that if we really wanted a baby that we should go home right then and have sex. The time was right to try again. We were assured that the miscarriage would have no bearing on another pregnancy. I had come to her thinking I had to have a hysterectomy, and was leaving with newfound confidence, as well as a second chance for a baby. It must have been fate that I saw her that day. I'll always believe that it was.

As we walked to the car both of us were giddy with excitement all the way home. We made love as the doctor instructed several times over the next days. Even if nothing came of it, we were sure having fun trying.

Then one afternoon Mark was in the kitchen cooking something that contained garlic. Garlic had always been one of my greatest passions. But not that day. A queasy feeling quickly came over me, sending me racing to the bathroom where I threw up. I just knew I had to be pregnant. Mark took off immediately for the closest drug store and bought a home pregnancy test. We were thrilled when it showed a faint purple line in the test window. Our spirits were rising. I called Dr. Ames immediately. She wanted me to come in for a blood test. In my joyful state we drove there and I took the test. A few hours later she called to tell me that my HCG level was nine. A level of ten meant pregnancy for sure. The doctor called in a prescription for prenatal vitamins and told me to come back in two days for another blood test. Returning when the two painfully long days had passed, I was overjoyed to learn I was pregnant again.

Nevertheless, pregnancy after a miscarriage is very stressful. Each little twinge strikes fear in your heart. It took a lot of effort to shake off these negative thoughts, but each day that I was still pregnant made the next day a little easier to get through. My pregnancy began in late July. In August, we planned to take Tommy and Bobby home to visit their mother. Our new attorney thought it would be a gesture of goodwill toward Gayle. Mr. Warner felt it would help our case in court if we made it clear that we wanted the children to maintain a relationship with their birth mother. Mark would get a chance to meet with our new lawyer while we were there and help things along. Moreover, Maine was home to Mark. So many times, he had told me many wonderful things about growing up there. Seeing it for myself would open up a part of Mark's life to me. I liked that idea.

However, when we told Tommy about the trip, he begged us not to take him back there. The days prior to the trip were miserable. They were filled with Tommy's screaming fits. He went around urinating on everything: floors, walls, toys, beds, and anything else he could think of. By the time we left, I was totally exhausted. In addition, morning sickness was dogging me badly and lasting throughout the whole day. In a strange way, this was comforting, because I knew it meant that the hormone levels were high enough in my body to support the pregnancy. We stopped at my mom's for a couple of days and let Jeff, who didn't want to drive all the way to Maine, stay there. I hated not having him with us, but knew he'd have a good time.

The trip was long and wearing. Between feeling sick and the kids acting up, I just wanted to get the trip over with. We had planned to drive straight through, but after twelve tedious hours, we stopped in Pennsylvania for the night. At six the next morning, we got back on the road and soon hit the state line.

Mark and I stayed at a small inn near Mark's parents. The children were staying at the homes of both Will and Alice and Mark's parents. Kyle and Jessica were thrilled to be seeing their "newly adopted" grandparents again. You can never have too many grandparents! The more you have, the luckier you are!

Mark's hometown, buried deep in the surrounding tree-covered mountains, was sleepy and far removed from the hustle and bustle of city life. The scenery was breathtaking, green as far as the eye could see. The clouds seemed to crown the top of the mountains, giving the illusion that you could almost reach up and touch them. Victorian houses lined the streets, some rundown, some restored, giving the city a homey kind of charm. The nearest Wal-Mart was an hour away. Though I missed the conveniences, it was easy to understand why Mark loved Maine. This small town was a bit of heaven on earth.

Shortly after we arrived we went to see Will and Alice. Gayle and her brother were visiting also. Alice's home was especially warm and inviting. Everyone who crossed the threshold was treated cordially and even their dog was super friendly. They had a way of making everyone feel right at home, especially my children and me.

Our pleasant visit ended when Tommy approached his mother and immediately began telling her what Rod had done to him. The room grew dead silent while we waited for Gayle's response to the allegations. When she insisted, "No honey, he didn't," we were all left speechless with shock. I wondered how a mother could not believe her own child. I knew Tommy's story had remained consistent since day one. As he began crying, I felt sick. I turned to Mark, who was visibly angry, and he squeezed my hand tightly to let me know he was there. Mark's self-control is amazing. I knew he wanted to tell Gayle that she was wrong, but he held his tongue. Later, he told me that he had actually bitten a chunk off the side of his tongue, while clenching his teeth to keep from saying anything. "I had to keep quiet. I didn't dare endanger our custody case. Protecting Tommy and Bobby is the most important thing." Endangering our case would definitely endanger them. All we could do now was try to exercise damage control. After Gayle left we told Tommy how proud we were that he told his mother the truth about Rod. Tommy looked at us with sad eyes and said, "But she didn't believe me." Our hearts broke for him.

The next day, Mark and I went to meet with our new lawyer, Mr. Warner. Mark and I laid our concerns before him. He told us that if Gayle wanted to take the boys to her house to visit, she had that right. We couldn't refuse without serious legal problems. That terrified us, as Rod lived in the same house. "Why doesn't the law protect these children?" I asked, unable to keep my voice from breaking with emotion. "We want a restraining order against Rod having any contact with the boys, during our visit or ever, for that matter." Mr. Warner was against that move. In hindsight, it may have opened the custody judge's eyes to the reality of the situation.

Mr. Warner didn't seem to like me very much. I guess it was

because I was very emotional. Maybe it was because, in my desperation to tell him everything, I kept interrupting him. I have Attention Deficit/Hyperactivity Disorder like my son, Jeff, and have a tendency to interrupt people when I get excited. I'm not intentionally trying to be rude. My train of thought derails very easily when I am stressed or upset.

However, Mark seemed to like Mr. Warner a lot. The lawyer's own confidence in his abilities was obvious. For some reason, the natural assumption is that high-priced lawyers are the best lawyers. But it's my opinion that this is not always the case. Todd had been really reasonably priced and not only was he extremely competent, but we completely trusted him. My gut feeling was that this guy wasn't the right guy for us, but I shut my mouth. Mark's dad was paying him a king's ransom and I was very grateful for his help. We really needed it. It made me mad that Mark didn't defend me, but I knew he felt similarly. Mark must have felt intimidated by this larger-than-life lawyer. I certainly was.

Gayle arrived at her parent's house the next afternoon while we were still there. Alice and Will were in the backyard with the kids, swimming. Gayle took her daughter and went outside to the pool. I stayed as far away from her as I physically could. While she was outside, I got a chance to meet her older brother and his wife. Her brother was very handsome and muscular, with a mischievous twinkle in his eye that you could see a mile away. He was warm and friendly to my kids and me. I was grateful for his friendliness. I had been warned that his wife probably wouldn't like me, because she was loyal to Gayle. Her total graciousness toward me came as a surprise. She was sweet to me and I really liked her and their two children.

A few days after our arrival in Maine, wanting to do something the children would enjoy, we took a day trip to a local amusement park, Santa's Village. Everyone had a good time, but when we returned home, Tommy began crying and screaming he didn't want to see his mother again. Alice was able to calm him down and make him feel better. That was the effect that she had on me as well. Her mothering nature was strong. You felt safe in her presence. Mark and I were grateful that she was there to comfort Tommy.

The next day Gayle's dad and older brother went with Mark to the races. He needed some time out from all the stress we had been experiencing. I tried to put on a brave front at the thought of him not being there when Gayle visited that afternoon, but inside I wanted to cry at the thought of being left alone with her. Kissing him goodbye made me feel like I was being thrown to the sharks. My stomach was churning and I couldn't eat at all that morning. Gayle's younger brother needed to study for a driver's license exam and I gratefully accepted his request that I help him study for it. Being with him kept my mind off Gayle's impending visit. When she came over we kept on studying and I made no attempt to join her in the kitchen or to interact with her in any way. I still couldn't accept how she denied what was obviously the painful truth that Tommy had told her. Her reaction did not reconcile with my ideas of the responsibilities of motherhood. Finally she left and I sat down trying to quiet my distress and was happy to see Mark arriving.

The peacefulness of the evening suddenly was pierced by Tommy's screams when he fell and bumped his head jumping on the living room furniture. I ran in to see it was no big deal, just your average kid booboo. Holding him in my arms, I tried to comfort him. He responded by quickly calming down. However, as his mother walked in the front door, Tommy leapt out of my lap and began screaming at the top of his lungs. He ran to her to show her his bump. My heart sank to my feet as he begged her for a Band-Aid. She acted concerned. What really crushed me the most was the fact that Tommy ran to her as if I didn't exist. In my heart, I wanted him to run to me with his wound and ask for me to fix it. At that moment, I knew that no matter how hard I tried to give him love, he would still always be desperate for hers. This was something about which I felt badly, though I could readily understand. A child's need for his mother's love is irreplaceable.

On our last evening in Maine we celebrated Mark's birthday at Will and Alice's. Mark's parents, their sons and grandsons were all there. We had a delicious dinner and the party meant so much to my husband. I could see coming back home had done him a lot of good. Spending time with his parents and Will and Alice had helped Mark heal old hurts and form closer ties with extended family. Also, we had time alone at the bed-and-breakfast for the first time since we had married. It was blissful. And we felt we had succeeded in protecting Mark's boys as much as we possibly could. Everyone felt relieved that no further harm had come to them. Or had it?

– c h a p t e r   f i v e –

Complications

Back home, the stresses of our lives multiplied. Tommy's behavior was growing more and more disturbing and things were beginning to go wrong with my pregnancy. When I was fourteen weeks along, we were told that my alpha-fetal protein test had been positive for Down syndrome. I refused to have an amniocentesis to either confirm or deny this conclusion, because there was a risk of miscarriage. Mark and I both wanted our child, physically challenged or not. The frustration of seeing two children born normal and damaged by abuse and neglect was the most intense pain we had ever experienced. If our baby was born with Down Syndrome, we would accept it just the way it was. Whatever child God sent to us we would love.

Meanwhile, with each passing day we grew more worried about the ways Tommy was acting out. He was sticking his hands inside of Bobby's pants and playing with his penis. Bobby, being totally passive, would let him. When I caught Tommy in the act and told him his behavior was inappropriate, he always acted shocked. His sexualized behavior didn't end. One day he sat down at the computer to play a game with Jeff. While Jeff was concentrating on the game, Tommy used his fingers to "walk" up Jeff's thigh, and started rubbing Jeff's penis through his shorts. Jeff turned white as a ghost. He picked Tommy up, holding him away from his body and carried him to our room. Jeff was stuttering as he tried to tell us what Tommy did to him. You could see that he was totally mortified. We disciplined Tommy by sending him to his room. Then we both went to him and gave him a lengthy explanation of why what he had done was wrong. At first he laughed, then he just stared at us.

It wasn't too long after touching Jeff that Tommy grabbed Jessica's crotch while the two of them were sitting together watching a television show. She came to me crying and in a panic. Tommy was disciplined again, but to no avail. He even did the same thing to me. Tommy had come in to say goodnight while I was lying on my bed reading. Before I even realized what had happened, he had stuck his hand between my legs, grabbing my genital area and squeezing. Stunned, I sent him to his room. I was becoming more agonized that we couldn't seem to change Tommy's inappropriate behavior no matter what measures we applied. Was it really possible for a child so young to be this disturbed?

The other children were justifiably appalled by the things he was doing. They didn't want to be around him. Lonely and miserable, he acted out in even more bizarre ways. Tommy's counselor Robin suspected that there was more to his stories of severe abuse, but didn't dare push Tommy too hard for details. He was only five. We just had to wait and see.

As the tension built, my blood pressure began to climb ominously and I had heart palpitations. My head ached and I couldn't eat. Worry was all I could seem to feel. As if I needed any more anxiety, a new ultrasound to look for further signs of Down Syndrome now revealed that the baby had a serious medical condition in which a hole develops in the heart. Never had I been so fearful.

Along with my anxiety about Tommy and Bobby, now I had to face the fact that I could be having a baby who might not only be mentally challenged but with serious physical problems. How were we going to make it through all this? If the baby's heart didn't mend itself, and the doctor said this was an unlikely possibility, the infant would probably need emergency surgery to repair it. The baby would need extra care after surgery. With Tommy and Bobby's needs absorbing my whole life, how was I going to be able to take care of a critically ill baby, too?

Mark and I were terrified. I prayed every day that my baby would be born healthy. I told myself there was always a chance that, by some miracle, the hole in the baby's heart would close before birth. Mark and I had said when I found out I was pregnant that no matter what problems the baby had, we would love the child. We just knew that our love for this baby would pull us through.

The baby was a boy. The doctor had shown us during the last ultrasound. Knowing the sex of the child made him seem all the more real to us. Trying to concentrate on the positive rather than our fears, we wracked our brains trying to come up with just the right name for him. Finally, we decided to name him Jacob. Jake sounded like a strong and confident name to me. With the odds already stacked against him, giving our baby a strong name seemed very important. His middle name would be Mark, like his father. More than anything I wanted our child to be normal, especially for Mark. We feared Tommy and Bobby's problems were so serious that it made their futures uncertain. At this point we still didn't know how bad the damage done to the boys was or if it could ever be repaired. We were trying as hard as we could to make them feel secure and loved, but could not help agonizing over whether they would be able to lead productive lives. Would they ever live independently, get married or have children of their own? My husband deserved some joy in his life again. I prayed Jake would be that joy.

In addition to nervousness about the boys, every day I worried about my baby and the impending custody case. That fall, the judge in Maine finally scheduled the custody case. I took care of the children while Mark went to Maine. Dealing with Tommy's tantrums while alone and pregnant was exhausting. I knew my husband needed me and was sad that I couldn't be there supporting him. I was glad that Will, Alice, Bob and Perry all decided to go to court on Mark's behalf. In a remarkable show of resolve, they sought to protect their beloved grandchildren together. I know it must have been tremendously difficult for Will and Alice to stand up against their own daughter. However, what had happened to their grandchildren had devastated them. They wanted more than anything for the two boys to be safe.

The day of the hearing I paced the floor, waiting for Mark's call. Finally, when the phone rang, Mark informed me that the judge was not going to make his decision that day. I felt overwhelmed with emotion and I quickly hung up. To this day, I regret that I didn't try to comfort my husband. Instead, overcome by my own intense pain, I raced to the bathroom so the children wouldn't hear me. Weeping uncontrollably, I released my agony. Months and months of pent-up stress flowed out of me. I felt furious at the judge for not immediately seeing the truth and the danger. For the first time, the boys had two parents who loved them, brothers and a sister, a stable home, security. They were safe! Why did the judge need time to decide where they needed to be? Didn't he see what was best in court that day? What was wrong with him? I learned later that night when Mark called back that our lawyer thought it best not to bring up the abuse charges in detail at the hearing. I personally thought that was a bad mistake, but I wasn't a lawyer. I was just a concerned stepmother with an uneasy feeling.

As we waited in agony for a decision about the boys' custody, Tommy's PTSD was getting progressively worse. Seeing his mother in Maine had brought back additional traumatic memories. We saw a counselor once a week with him, but nothing was improving. He was constantly urinating all over the walls and carpet in the house. He was smearing feces in his bedroom almost daily. The smell permeating our home was just awful. The padding underneath the carpet had absorbed the urine, making the odor impossible to conceal. In addition to this behavior Tommy had begun cursing at Jessica and me a lot. He seemed especially resentful of my pregnancy. One day he got a running start, with both arms extended in front of him and rammed my belly full force with his fists. He just stood there, grinning as I doubled over in pain. I was beginning to be fearful of what he might actually do after the baby was born.

Presently, however our thoughts were focusing on protecting ourselves from him. While it was hard to believe we were afraid of a small child, it was true. We searched the house for anything that could be used as a weapon. We hid objects. We put all the knives on the highest shelf in the kitchen, hidden from sight. We did the same thing with matches and the wood stove lighter. Anything we could perceive

Tommy might wield against us was put away. Our dread was growing deeper every day. By this time we saw there was rage boiling inside him, and were terrified that one day he would explode. What further secrets were stoking the fire under Tommy's rage? I kept telling myself that he was only five. Feeling frightened of a five-year-old was embarrassing. Five-year-olds were supposed to be curious, not dangerous. I still felt that if I just loved him more, if my love could just infuse him, he would somehow get over all of this and be fine. Never one to give up, I strengthened my resolve to keep trying, even in the face of growing fear.

Thanksgiving and Christmas passed. Their mother did not send the boys presents. I could see they felt upset and rejected. We tried to make it up to them by making the Christmas season special. Since they had come with no toys we figured that now was the time to indulge them a little. The grandparents seemed to be thinking the same thing. They spoiled all five of the kids with lovely things and loving wishes. There was still no ruling and we tried not to worry about the judge's decision in the custody case, but it was always in the background. The general consensus was that things must have been going our way, since the judge hadn't made the boys go back to Gayle's for Christmas.

One cold January afternoon, not too long after the holidays, I wasn't feeling too well. I drove to Dr. Ames' office alone for my checkup. As I sat in the waiting room, Mark suddenly walked in. Taken aback, I immediately began to question what he was doing there. "You're supposed to be at work." Mark took my hands in his. As gently as he could, he told me the judge had ruled that the children had to be returned to Gayle. I began sobbing loudly. Dr. Ames came to get me, saying, "Mark, she has to remain as calm as possible, for the baby's sake." That was impossible. Returning home, I headed straight for bed. We both cried for a long time and, when we finally calmed down, Mark and I called both grandparents. They were as shocked by the ruling as we were.

Immediately, our lawyer filed paperwork to get the judge to reconsider. Nevertheless, about a month later, we again were ordered to return the children. The judge in Maine stated that he would look at the abuse charges after the children were returned. Mark asked Mr. Warner if there was any way the case could be brought to Virginia. He told

Mark that we didn't want to do that. By this time my early negative feelings about our lawyer returned. He had advised us against the restraining order and didn't want to accuse Gayle of abuse at the previous custody hearing. We felt he wasn't giving us good counsel, but we were in too deep to go back. We were searching for answers. What should we do? There had to be a way to protect these kids, but how?

When we talked to Gayle's mother, she gave us the most valuable advice we would ever get. She told Mark to go see a lawyer in Virginia and have the lawyer ask the courts to have the custody hearing in Virginia. After all, the children's counselor and doctors were there. Bobby had been seeing a pediatric specialist for his "severe malnutrition due to maternal neglect" for several months. Her testimony, and that of their counselor, Robin, were absolutely crucial to proving our case. Neither of them had been able to travel to Maine for the hearing. Moving the case to Virginia made a lot of sense. Heeding his former mother-in-law's advice, Mark picked a lawyer at random from the phone book. The angels must have been guiding him that day, because he picked a winner.

The new lawyer's name was Tom Taylor. Mark went to see him the next afternoon. We were scared to death that he might not be able to help us. Our financial situation was becoming more critical by the day and we were afraid a new lawyer would require another retainer and more monthly payments. We were already sinking from all the bills, including the ones for Tommy's and Bobby's counseling. How could we possibly take on any more? On the other hand, we felt we had to do the right thing for the boys no matter what it cost.

At that first meeting Tom listened patiently to Mark and then came up with an immediate plan. He said that, because the kids had been here over six months, Virginia was actually entitled to jurisdiction over the case. He brought Mark before Judge Stone the next day. The judge immediately decided to take jurisdiction of the case.

However, the judge in Maine proceeded to take steps to stop Judge Stone's action. Nevertheless, Judge Stone's supervisors backed up his decision to hear the case in Virginia.

Gayle was notified of the impending hearing. She was also notified that she needed to contact the Department of Social Services in Maine for a home study. This had to be completed before the custody hearing.

We were to be investigated fully as well. We welcomed it. Our home study went great, with the caseworker even calling me afterwards. She told me that, "Yours is the nicest family I have ever done a study on," and said that the report on our family was the most glowing report she had ever written. Our hopes were beginning to soar.

The custody hearing in Virginia was held a couple of weeks later. Mark's parents, as well as Gayle's, came with us. Once again Gayle did not appear. Not wanting to make a judgment without at least giving her one more chance to appear, Judge Stone set a new court date. The bright spot in all of this was that we got to see our favorite people again. Nevertheless, I felt badly that they had to come so far for nothing, but just having all four grandparents with us was very comforting.

Gayle's attorney secured a lawyer for her in Virginia. Judge Stone had appointed a guardian ad litem, Rose Morton, for the boys. She talked to Gayle and to us as well. Ms. Morton's job was to represent the boys' best interests in the case. We prayed she would find out the truth through the home study scheduled for Gayle.

Meanwhile, the stress was really getting to me. My blood pressure was now consistently high and I was running the risk of developing toxemia again. Dr. Ames called me her "problem child." When I was thirty-two weeks pregnant; she tried to start me on Betamethasone, an injectable steroid that causes babies' lungs to mature more quickly, just in case the baby was born early. However, the steroids had to be stopped after the first injection caused me to have an allergic reaction. Keeping the baby inside me as long as possible was top priority so the doctor ordered bed rest.

But when I was thirty-six weeks along, I got a call that Tommy and Bobby needed to be picked up from their special-ed preschool. They were vomiting and running high fevers. Mark was almost an hour away and no one else could drive me there. I wasn't supposed to get out of bed, but what choice did I have? My belly huge, I could barely squeeze myself behind the wheel of the car. Just walking to the school office was a struggle. While I was picking them up, Mark had come home from work early. He was in a total panic when he saw the car gone and could not find me in the house. I hadn't left a note, because I didn't expect him home so early. He was just about to leave for the hospital, to see if I was there, when I pulled into the driveway. I was exhausted. Extremely upset and worried, he immediately rushed to me. Mark started fussing at me about how I had scared him. I felt really badly about that but explained that the boys had taken ill and the school called to pick them up. I sent the boys to bed as my husband continued venting his upset feelings. We were both stopped short when Tommy and Bobby began projectile vomiting all over the bathroom. Mark cleaned them up and put them to bed; I cleaned up the bathroom. That was a big mistake. Two days later the boys broke out in a lacy looking red rash all over their bodies. They had Fifth disease, one of those common childhood viruses. Unfortunately, it can be dangerous to pregnant women. In the first trimester, it can cause miscarriage. I was in the third trimester where it can cause severe anemia in the mother and in her child. "Dear God," I prayed, "please let my baby be fine. I have so much else to worry about."

chapter six

Life's Crazy Turns

The next day Dr. Ames tested me for Fifth disease. After finding out I didn't have it, she suggested that in view of my high blood pressure, etcetera, we plan a labor induction on her next hospital day. I was terrified at the thought of being induced, but liked the idea that I would be at the hospital when labor started, since I barely made it when Jessica was born.

On the scheduled morning, my nervousness caused me to begin regular contractions. We arrived at the designated time, seven-thirty A.M. I had asked Dr. Ames which hospital she thought would be best for labor, and she had said Chesapeake. Looking around I was glad we'd made this choice. My room was cheery and comfortable with a private bathroom and shower and there was furniture that made it look like a bedroom in a home, not a hospital room. There was even a television and a stereo. I felt as though I was being treated like royalty.

The nurses had to laugh when I gave them a list of all my past and present pregnancy complications. They said it was the longest list they had ever seen. Dr. Ames soon arrived and then the Pitocin was begun. It was given intravenously. She said Pitocin would cause me to go into active labor and that's precisely what it did.

The baby arrived quickly. As Dr. Ames did Jake's evaluation, she said that she detected no sign of Down Syndrome. The tension and nervousness over Jake's condition began to drain quickly from my body. However, it returned when Jake was not given to me to hold. Dr. Ames thought she heard a murmur. He was given immediately to a cardiac nurse to evaluate. My heart sank. My baby did not have its first bonding experience with me. My arms ached with emptiness. I knew the doctors were doing the right thing, but I wanted so badly to hold him.

Still, I couldn't wait to call Jessica and tell her that Jake was finally here. She had been my constant companion through the pregnancy. Her heart had been broken by my miscarriage. Now, she would finally have the baby brother she had hoped for. Kyle and Jeff had to wake her up for the news. She had fallen fast asleep fully dressed. Taking care of Tommy and Bobby all day had been exhausting for her, but she never complained.

When we brought Jake home we felt like this was a new beginning for us. Jake would be the glue that bonded the whole family, the tie that binds. All five children were related to the baby by blood. Suddenly, we were all bonded to each other because of this beautiful, blue-eyed boy. A cardiology appointment, two days after birth, revealed another miracle. The hole in Jake's heart had closed before birth. Our precious baby was perfect. We felt like the luckiest parents in the whole world.

Mark and I felt so solid. Our marriage was strong and we were filled with hope for the future.

Getting used to taking care of a small baby in addition to the other children was exhausting and Jake never seemed to be able to sleep. He always had copious amounts of mucus in his nose and throat. I suspected allergies because of his symptoms, but the doctors seemed to dismiss my concerns. Then on a routine visit to Dr. Ames, she heard Jake wheezing. He was only six weeks old. Her own five-year-old daughter had developed asthma at an early age. Dr. Ames had gone through many doctors dismissing her own concerns before her daughter had been diagnosed. Mother to mother, she understood my concerns and placed a call to Jake's pediatric group. They, of course, dismissed my concern that he had allergies or asthma, even with the information that Dr. Ames had provided. They said he was too young for allergies. Mark and I left frustrated.

After doing a lot of reading on allergies and infants, I began to suspect that he was allergic to breast milk. Jake was constantly having trouble breathing because of the mucus. In intervals of every fifteen minutes, all night long, I would suction his nose and cry my eyes out. Based on my research, I decided to follow my hunch and try him on soy formula, which is hypoallergenic. The change was apparent from the very first bottle I gave him. The congestion returned to normal levels. Because of the change in formula, he could sleep a couple of hours at a time between feedings. I guess that one of the best pieces of advice that I could give any mother is to follow your instincts when it comes to your children. Doctors may know about medicine, and I praise them for that, but mothers know their own children.

Jake was still a night owl, though, and I was getting more and more sleep deprived. My older son Jeffrey was a night owl, too. On the weekends and during the summer he often stayed up till very late. Jeffrey offered to sit up with his baby brother at night, so I could get some sleep. That was a most precious sight. They were truly bonding. Jeffrey did a great job of taking care of Jake. He was a little scared of the baby at first, but his confidence grew along with his love for his little brother. Soon, Jeff could change and feed Jake like a seasoned pro. All the older kids pitched in. Mark and I were grateful and proud of them. Seeing teenagers changing dirty diapers without complaint is an amazing and rare sight. They were growing up to be kind, loving and responsible people.

Though I loved taking care of the baby, it was taking care of Tommy and Bobby that took most of my time during the day. Tommy was having PTSD attacks almost daily and Bobby needed to be fed, dressed and cleaned up after his many bowel and bladder accidents. His potty training still was not going well.

One day to my horror, we caught Tommy trying to put his hands around Jake's throat so that he could choke him. I had only turned my back for a moment to tie Bobby's shoes. A few days after this incident, I was holding the baby when Tommy approached. Feeling certain that he wouldn't hurt Jake with me holding him, I allowed him to look at the baby a little closer, hoping to encourage their relationship. Tommy reached out his hand, as if to touch the baby's face. Then he clenched his teeth and he put his hand around the baby's throat. Immediately, I grabbed his hand and pushed it away. "No, Tommy. No. You must treat your brother gently." Tommy looked at me vacantly and walked away. "Dear God, please help me," I prayed. "Please help me."

My concern was increasing daily. Whenever Tommy was around the other children, I couldn't take my eyes off him for even a second. We were all on alert and growing more anxious about him with each passing day.

A week after he tried to choke the baby, Tommy walked into the living room. Jake was peacefully swinging in the baby swing. Tommy acted as though he was going across the room to watch television. However, as he started to pass the swing, without warning, he abruptly stopped beside it. Suddenly, he forcefully kicked the front leg of the swing, sending it toppling over. Luckily, I was close to the swing. As it began to fall, I jumped up and grabbed it. Averting potential tragedy, I just stared at Tommy, my heart racing anxiously. Tommy just smiled as once again I tried to explain why he couldn't be so wild around the baby. I was growing more and more afraid.

Not long after this we got notice that the court case would be held in mid-April. Once again, Mark's parents and Will and Alice came down from Maine for the hearing. Alice told us a friend had informed her that Gayle and Rod had been seen leaving town with a fully packed car. This was upsetting, to say the least. Had she finally decided to come down to Virginia and fight for her kids? Was there a chance that we might have to give them back to her? We felt confident in our lawyer's abilities, but with custody cases anything can happen in court. You never know for sure. A part of me was almost glad that she was on her way to Virginia, in spite of my fears. Now, we would finally have the showdown we had been expecting for what seemed like an eternity.

The rest of our family was nervous as they left for court that morning. I was unable to attend, because I had to watch Tommy and Bobby. We didn't dare leave them with a babysitter because of Tommy's bizarre behavior. I wore a path in the carpet with my pacing. The hours seemed to stretch on forever with no word. Finally, I heard a car in the driveway. I raced anxiously for the front door. The look on everyone's faces was one of pure disgust. Questions rapidly poured from my mouth as I desperately tried to find out what had happened in court. Mark said Gayle had once again not shown up! "She sent a letter to the judge asking for a continuance. Judge Stone had no choice but to grant her request." Because of the Maine judge's complaints, he was making absolutely sure that things were done to the letter. He didn't want any mistakes. Judge Stone apologized to Mark, his parents and Gayle's parents. He rescheduled the hearing for late in May. He promised that on that date, all of this would finally be over.

I couldn't believe what I was hearing. In addition, Mark and I felt guilty that everyone had come so far from home to help us and, once again, nothing had happened. We seemed doomed to perpetual limbo. Depression was setting in, but we tried to hold to the hope that the next court date would be the last.

The days before the third hearing in court were filled with pressure and worry. We prayed that the final decision would be in our favor. Meanwhile, Tommy still was urinating all over the house and having continual tantrums. Mark and I both felt that if we could just win custody, time, counseling and our love for Tommy and Bobby would eventually help the boys overcome their emotional problems.

Bobby was looking so much better now, but still seemed stuck in perpetual infancy. He was cute, sweet and responded to affection. Tommy continued to sporadically reveal more about the abuse and my heart just went out to him and Bobby. I wanted more than anything to just fix everything for those two children. I still had faith that the power of love would eventually make everything okay for them. Many nights, I would lie awake for hours praying. My prayers were that God would show me what to do to help them. Time and time again, in the darkness, I tried to analyze the situation. Many times, I came up with new methods to try to help Tommy and Bobby. Disappointingly none of them seemed to be very effective.

Tommy's rage seemed to grow deeper and stronger. No one could blame him, considering what he and Bobby had gone through. However, feelings of helplessness haunted me day after day as I tried to help him deal with his feelings. Quitting was not an option for me.

Our day in court finally arrived. Kissing Mark and the others goodbye as they left, I had a sick feeling in my stomach. At hand was the moment that would define the future of these two little boys. We believed sending them back to their mother would end any hope that they could be healed. Even with the children's serious problems, Mark and I loved them dearly and were committed to giving them the best possible life. I prayed hard that they would be ours. As I waited, I talked out loud to God; asking him to please let us keep the children. "Please God, just give me the chance to help these children. I know you sent them to me because you knew I wouldn't give up, no matter how hard it gets. Please, just give me the chance."

The past year flashed through my mind, reminding me of how much we had been through as a family. We had suffered so much to get to this moment and now it was upon us. Each minute ticking by seemed slow and painful as I waited and waited for the news.

Finally I heard the front door opening and rushing there, I was greeted by the beautiful, glowing, triumphant smiles of Mark, his parent's and Will and Alice. We had won! Gayle had once again not shown up. The judge taking note of the fact that there was, according to the social worker's report, evidence of abuse and neglect, had given Gayle only supervised visitation, which meant that she had to have someone present from the Department of Social Services when she saw or telephoned the boys. We weren't exactly happy about that part, but without a full-blown abuse hearing against Gayle taking place, there was no way the judge could just remove her parental rights. The D.S.S. would charge her a fee to be present during visits and calls.

Gayle never called the children again. No birthday cards, Christmas presents or letters were ever sent to the children after the court date. As long as I live, I'll never be able to understand.

Our mood at the steakhouse where we went to celebrate was one of elation. Everyone rejoiced. We all thought that our troubles were finally going to be over. Gayle and the judge in Maine had other ideas. The judge in Maine was totally irate about the custody being awarded in Virginia and not by him. Gayle's lawyer in Maine asked that contempt of court charges be filed against Mark for not returning the children as the Maine judge had ordered. They also asked that we pay for her lawyer's fees in the case, although we knew her lawyer was working for her pro bono. Not long after our victory in court, the judge in Maine filed a new order, ordering that Mark be fined five hundred dollars a day for every day he didn't return the children to Maine for a new hearing. Mark and I were absolutely terrified. The fine for one year would have been six times Mark's annual salary. The order also stated the judge could issue a warrant for Mark's arrest for contempt of court if Mark came back to Maine. With his mother's declining health, this was the ultimate hurt for Mark. He wouldn't be able to visit his parents any more. We all knew there would come a day when his mother couldn't travel anymore. When that day came, we were afraid Mark would never see her again. That was too painful to imagine. However, we also felt there was no question that we were keeping the children, in spite of the painful issues. We had come this far and we weren't going back. My husband was taking a stand for his children. I was so very proud of him.

After a careful review, our new attorney thought that he could eventually get the charges dropped, but it was definitely going to cost us. Emotionally, we were exhausted and weren't up to even a small fight, much less the tremendous battle we faced. Thank God for earthly angels! Thank God for Alice! Never one to take things lying down, she wrote a very detailed letter to the Maine State Attorney General, asking him to look into the matter. Based on Alice's complaint, the attorney general began investigating the case. A few weeks later we got notice that the contempt charge had been dropped and the judge reprimanded. Our new attorney still had to go to court over the legal fees for Gayle's attorney, but that matter was quickly dropped. It had cost us a few thousand dollars, but once again, we were feeling elated and looking forward to moving on with our lives. The boys were out of a nightmarish situation and that was all that mattered to us.

chapter seven

Sinking Into Madness

Our joyous feeling after the custody hearing and the end of the trouble that followed, didn't last long. Tommy began revealing even more truly horrifying information about his past abuse and his PTSD attacks were escalating. With each day that passed my stepson described more of the horror he had suffered. He described how feces were put in his breakfast cereal, and repeated his stories of the sexual abuse he suffered at the hands of his caretakers. Since Tommy was reliving the sexual abuse almost every day, the more he remembered, the worse he got.

Each time Tommy disclosed a new dark revelation it came like a crashing wave of emotion that threw our lives into even more turmoil. We couldn't understand how such abhorrent evil had been perpetrated on innocent children.

After his painful revelations surfaced, we always made sure that we reassured Tommy that we believed him and loved him. We constantly assured him that nothing like that was ever going to happen to him again. We told him we would protect him and Bobby no matter what. In an attempt to comfort Tommy, I talked to him about the angels that love and watched over him, I spoke about God and His love for Tommy. I desperately wanted the child to have some sense of personal safety. At night, sitting on his bed telling Tommy good night, I tried to comfort him, "An angel sits on the foot of your bed. The angel is kind and will keep you safe from ever being harmed again." That seemed to offer him only temporary comfort, but I felt that was better than no comfort. In my heart, I knew I was telling him the truth about the angels. After what these children had survived, there had to be angels watching over them. That was something I just knew in my heart.

However, Tommy in his agony was acting out more and more outrageously. He had begun spitting on children in preschool and was becoming increasingly aggressive. Tommy bit a child at school. He constantly told us about a child who was picking on him during class. When I called this to his teacher's attention, she told us that the child that Tommy was talking about never teased anyone and was extremely passive. She told us that Tommy was the one picking on the other child.

His nervousness and rage seemed to be growing more serious every day. He was exhibiting tics when he was upset. He cleared his throat constantly in an exaggerated manner. He picked on areas of his arms and face until the skin literally came off, leaving large scabs. As I watched Tommy's eyes blinking over and over I began to think that there might be something neurologically wrong with him, even though the Navy specialist had not found brain damage. Tommy's body movements were becoming more noticeably spastic and he developed a very odd, almost ape-like, walk.

We were sick at heart that neither we nor those we consulted had helped Tommy who, by mid-July, seemed to be increasingly out of touch with reality, reliving the horrors he had lived through. We all made a point of not mentioning the abuse in front of Tommy and Bobby. We hoped that by not dwelling on it and focusing our attention on more positive things, eventually Tommy would begin to heal. It didn't help. Every day, he relived his trauma as if he was stuck in a time warp. It was as if he was frozen in a world so cold that he couldn't feel the warmth of the safety and love that surrounded him. He was physically with us, but mentally still living in the past.

Summer was upon us. The change in routine made Tommy agitated and angry about the break from school. His tantrums were getting increasingly violent. One day, while Tommy was playing outside with Jessica and her girlfriend, Tommy stood up, pulled down his pants, grabbed his penis and started wiggling it at the girls. He walked toward them and kept repeating, "I'm a bad boy."

I knew then we had to find a professional who specialized in childhood mental disorders. In tears, I called our insurance company for approval for Tommy to see a psychiatrist. He and Bobby had been in counseling since we originally got custody, but we felt he needed more intense help from a medical doctor who could prescribe medication. My voice was cracking with emotion as I called the psychiatrist's office. The receptionist was extremely kind and understanding. "We have to find out what is wrong with Tommy," I explained. "We're exhausted and have tried everything we know of to help him. None of it has seemed to help." She noted the urgency in my voice and said that Tommy could come in the next day.

We were on pins and needles when we met with Dr. Benson the next afternoon. However, the petite blond woman with very soft facial features was one of those people who immediately make you feel at ease. She had a gentleness about her that made you trust her from the start. There was a sense of comfort as we settled in to tell our story.

After talking with Tommy she offered a tentative diagnosis, Post-Traumatic Stress Disorder and ADHD. We were given a prescription for Ritalin. Maybe that was all he needed to slow down, we told ourselves. Therapy could surely help him deal with the abuse issues. Mark and I both breathed a sigh of relief that day. Maybe now things would finally get better.

However, two days after starting on Ritalin, Tommy's recurring tics became worse. He couldn't stop blinking his eyes, scratching his arms and clearing his throat. He couldn't control the spastic jerking of his body which now became more and more frequent. Moreover, Tommy seemed agitated and even moodier than usual. My heart was starting to sink. I tried to ignore the worsening of his behavior for a couple of days thinking his symptoms would get better as his body adjusted to the medicine. Then Tommy did something I could not ignore.

Going in to check on him while he was taking a nap, I gasped. He had twisted his bed sheet like a rope and wrapped it tightly around his throat. My eyes didn't want to believe what they were seeing. Tommy was lying silent on the bed, the sheet already cutting off his air, twisting the "rope" even tighter. Tommy fought me as I struggled to unwrap the sheet. Taking the sheet with me, I left the room in a total panic, I called Dr. Benson. She told me to stop the Ritalin immediately and bring Tommy in for an appointment. I was scared, really scared. What was happening to this child? How could a five-year-old possibly want to die? Why had he reacted so strongly to a relatively safe medication? Was there more wrong with him than we knew?

At our appointment the next day Dr. Benson put Tommy on antidepressants. Again, Mark and I felt a sense of renewed optimism. However, Tommy didn't calm down. Instead, the medication seemed to remove his inhibitions and increase his aggressiveness. With no provocation, Tommy now was attacking Jessica and me on a regular basis. Dr. Benson explained that Tommy seemed to harbor deep anger toward women, presumably based on his mother's treatment of him. His anger toward women would, naturally, be taken out on the easiest to hurt, i.e. the smallest female target in the house. She also explained that, while Tommy loved me for trying to be a good mother to him, he also hated me not only because I was female, but being a loving mother only served to show him the qualities his own mother was severely lacking. This motivated further anger toward me.

My heart ached for Jessica. She was trying so hard to fulfill the "big sister" role. When school started, she volunteered to watch Tommy at the bus stop. We didn't know then this would be a potentially tragic decision.

Tommy began the year in "the honeymoon" period with his new teacher, Miss Jones, who was young, naïve and unmarried and had no experience with a seriously disturbed child like Tommy. We had met with school officials prior to the start of school. During the meeting, Mark and I outlined Tommy's problems at home and at his previous school. At first everything seemed fine. Tommy was as loving to Miss Jones as he'd been to me. I had taught him to say "Yes ma'am" and "No ma'am." We knew, however, that eventually, when he figured out what an adult's limits were, he would begin acting out. He had already done this with his psychiatrist, counselor and his previous teacher.

A few weeks after school started, Tommy went to an assembly for the entire elementary school. During the program, he ran up on stage and lay down on the floor flapping his arms and legs as if he was swimming. Miss Jones called and told me about the incident. I apologized for his behavior, reminding her he was seeing a psychiatrist weekly and that we were doing all we could. A week later another disturbing incident occurred in the bathroom. Tommy walked into the boy's bathroom and, for some inexplicable reason, punched a second grade student in the jaw. Witnesses to the incident said it was totally unprovoked. The poor second grade boy was stunned at being attacked by a kindergartner for no reason. Shocked at the blow, he went straight to his teacher to report the attack. I got a note from Miss Jones giving me the details of the incident. Though I tried to explain the depth of Tommy's problems, she did not see the warning signs Tommy was giving her.

The children had become so withdrawn and upset over Tommy's continually bizarre behaviors, they didn't want their friends to come to the house any more, simply because they feared that Tommy would do something horrible in front of them. Jeff, Kyle and Jessica were also afraid to leave me at home alone with Tommy. They were scared that he would hurt the baby or me. Getting them to leave for school each morning had become a chore. Constantly, I had to reassure them that I was an adult and could protect the baby and myself from Tommy's violence, but they always left for school with sad looks on their faces. It broke my heart to see the effect that Tommy and Bobby's problems were having on the other children's lives.

After about six weeks in half-day kindergarten and half-day special-ed, it was decided to cut Tommy down to a half-day of regular kindergarten. The special-ed teacher would still monitor his progress. Mark and I were extremely upset. We talked with Dr. Benson about our concerns. She sent the school her recommendation that Tommy's routine not be changed, because it would cause him further emotional disturbance.

Mark and I called for a meeting with his teachers to try and beg them to understand Tommy's need for a stable routine. Mark was unable to attend when we finally scheduled a meeting, so I went alone. I tried hard to explain what would happen if they rocked Tommy's emotional boat, but, apparently because of budgetary problems, Tommy was going to be dropped from the half-day special-ed program. We were given no choice in the matter. I cried all the way home. We had tried so hard to form a working partnership with the school in order to help Tommy.

When Tommy was told about the change, he trashed his room, broke toys and threw things at us. He lay on his bed, kicking the walls for an hour. The whole house vibrated from his assault.

Dr. Benson had been steadily increasing Tommy's medication. She had even added some new ones for aggression. Nothing was stopping his increasingly violent outbursts. The day after we told him of the change at school, the real terror began.

That next morning I sent Jessica out with Tommy to wait for the bus to take them to school as usual. She always looked out for him as they waited together each day. However, a few minutes later a heart-stopping scream pierced the cool autumn air. Jessica ran into the house breathlessly, with her hand clutched over her heart. She was crying hysterically "Tommy stabbed me in the chest with a pair of scissors." Quickly I drew up her shirt and gasped. There was a bruise forming right near her heart. Jessica had picked up the scissors, as Tommy dropped them, and she handed them to me. Later we found out Tommy had stolen the metal scissors from his teacher's desk, hiding them deep in his book bag. He grabbed them from his bag, attacking Jessica. Luckily, the scissors had been round-tipped and only deeply bruised Jessica, who had been wearing a jacket. A protective angel must have been watching over my daughter that awful day.

I stared at Tommy in horror. Dear God, had what happened to Tommy turned him homicidal at five-years-old? He had stolen scissors and hidden them until he found an opportunity to attack Jessica. This was premeditated. The thought of his deviousness, no less his violent outburst, was horrifying. Trying to regain my composure, I called the school and told them what had happened. Then I wrote a hasty note to Miss Jones, again telling her that Tommy needed to be checked each day before he came home to make sure he had no sharp objects with him. Jessica was terribly shaken, but said she wanted to go on to school. I called Mark at work to tell him what happened. Then I collapsed into a sobbing heap on the floor. I had to pull myself together. I had a new infant to care for; Bobby was as helpless as a baby; and I had an extremely disturbed child that I couldn't seem to do anything to help. I felt like the weight of the Earth was bearing heavily down on my shoulders.

That afternoon, I got a note from Miss Jones in which she apologized for letting Tommy have access to the scissors. However, the school seemed to be blocking out Tommy's extremely disturbed behavior. Dr. Benson was beginning to suggest that if the behaviors continued to escalate, Tommy might need hospitalization to get stabilized. As parents, we really didn't want to take the hospitalization route until there seemed to be no other way. The thought of placing a five-year-old in a mental hospital was too painful.

We wanted to explore every other route to help him, so we were glad when Dr. Benson suggested taking him to a psychologist to have him evaluated developmentally. The school backed us up. Tommy, however, was becoming experienced at putting on a "cute" act for doctors. Tommy spent two days with Dr. Williams. On the last day of the evaluation, Dr. Williams asked Tommy and Jessica to wait in the outer office while he reviewed the results with us. Dr. Williams said Tommy had problems but saw no indication they were severe. After the meeting, I noticed that Jessica was holding her hand to her right eye as we walked to the car. After strapping everyone in, I situated myself in the front seat. When I turned around to make one last seat belt check on the kids, I was met by a horrible sight. There was a hole a quarter of an inch below Jessica's right bottom eyelid. Tommy had found a pencil in a toy box in Dr. William's waiting room and stabbed her under her eye. She hadn't even had time to react; he had acted too quickly. Mark and I were devastated. We disciplined Tommy again. We always disciplined him when he did something wrong, but despite this he would repeat the bad behavior, again and again. Mark and I had been counseled to be totally consistent with discipline, but it just didn't seem to be doing any good.

We called Dr. Benson with the news of Tommy's newest attack. As we had many times before, we took him in for an emergency appointment. He was now on massive doses of medication, yet they seemed to do nothing to stabilize him. Desperation was all we felt.

The change to a half-day school program was to begin. Tommy seemed to do okay the first day and he even got a "caught being good" award from Miss Jones. She sent him to the office. Unfortunately, they gave Tommy a pencil as an award. That afternoon on the bus, he tried to stab Jessica with it. Again, we placed a call to the school about giving him sharp objects. They agreed, yet again, to be more careful. Tommy was grounded. He spent the rest of the night shrieking and screaming. The walls shook from his kicks against them. When we went in to talk to him, Tommy was filled with rage. He directed his anger at us and at his teacher for taking away his special-ed program. Tommy was furious that he would now only see his usual teacher for a few minutes each day.

I thought we were in for more trouble, so I was pleasantly surprised on the afternoon after the change to half-day kindergarten, when I was alone with Tommy, Bobby and Jake. Things seemed to be running unusually smooth. Tommy was quiet. His calmness lulled me into a false sense of security. I found myself thinking that maybe I was wrong; maybe he could handle this change. Maybe he just needed to vent his anger at the situation to be able to accept it. I could only hope.

The quiet was soon shattered. Tommy began throwing things around in his room and cursing. Going to him, I calmly tried to reassure him that he could deal with the change. I tried to tell him that everything would be just fine. He began cursing me. There was no choice but to ground him. Before I left, I told him that he could come out of his room when he had calmed himself. The next hour was filled with his nerve-shattering screams. I could hear Tommy kicking even larger cracks in the drywall. The cracks were over a foot long now, as if they were growing along with his internal rage. Suddenly, there was silence. I was in the kitchen preparing a snack for Jake and Bobby. As I leaned up against the stove heating Jake's baby food, I sensed a presence behind me. Quickly turning, I saw Tommy standing beside me. He screamed, "I hate you, you fucking bitch!" He balled up his fist and slugged me. I tried to get my bearings as Tommy stormed off back to his room.

Shaking, I grabbed the phone to call Mark. Dissolving into grief-stricken tears, I told him that I had to call Dr. Benson and tell her what happened and ask her to hospitalize Tommy. He agreed. After I said good bye, I called her. Hearing my story, Dr. Benson agreed Tommy needed more therapy than we could give him at home. After talking to her I sat there thinking, *Have I done the right thing? Am I giving up? Could Tommy ever be helped? What else could we do at this point?*

Having a mentally ill family member is like climbing a never-ending spiral staircase. You feel like you are just going round and round in circles and are never really getting closer to help. You have lots of hopes that as you climb the staircase you are going to leave the illness behind, but the illness always seems to come back around to meet you at the next turn. It's just always there. The nature of the illness keeps it both behind and in front of you at the same time. Each step you take is plagued by the fears you have acquired from the steps you have just finished climbing. Even when the steps before you offer hope, the steps behind you, where you felt no hope whatsoever, stay in your mind. You just can't get away from it no matter how hard you try. You just keep going around and around…

–*c h a p t e r e i g h t*–

The Mental Hospital

In silence, Mark and I drove Tommy to the private psychiatric hospital. The cracks we could feel forming in our hearts were from the painful feeling of despair. We had tried everything humanly possible to help this child and it just wasn't enough. Both of us felt horrible guilt that it had come to this point, but we didn't know what else to do to help Tommy. Tommy didn't say a word, just sat in the backseat with an angry look in his eyes.

As we walked through the sliding glass doors into the hospital, I was struck by the peaceful feeling of the waiting area. The receptionist told us that she had been expecting us and we were soon ushered into an intake room. There, we talked for over an hour to the intake person. We explained the details of Tommy's abusive history, his current level of psychiatric care and his present violent behaviors. It was after seven in the evening when we finally were escorted to the locked ward upstairs to admit Tommy.

At that point Tommy's bag of clothing was taken from us and searched. All character T-shirts were sent back home with us. Robe ties and drawstrings from pants were removed. They required that my pocketbook be left at the desk. I felt uncomfortable at the invasion of my privacy. My purse was always something I kept with me and now it was both searched and then taken from me. The reason behind this made perfect sense; they were keeping dangerous items from very sick children. Still, it made me feel like I was a prisoner.

Tommy told us goodbye as if he didn't even care if we left him or not. That hurt a lot. As the steel door locked behind us when we left, I started to cry. I felt like a complete failure. My father had always raised me to be a "never-quitter." Now, I felt like I had failed at doing my job of helping Tommy, as I had promised Mark and his family that I would. As hard as I had tried, I just couldn't do it. Now, someone else had to step in and try. It felt like I had been fired. He needed a certain level of care and I just couldn't provide this; the hospital had to.

Mark offered me as much comfort as he could muster on the drive home. He said that he was feeling much the same as I was. Tears streamed silently from my eyes all the way. The calls we placed to his parents and Will and Alice that night were extremely painful. I broke down and cried. Alice did her best to reassure me, gently pointing out that some problems just can't be fixed with love. My mother also repeated the same sentiments when I talked to her later, offering me great comfort. A part of me knew that they were absolutely right, but a part of me just didn't want to believe that I couldn't do anything to fix Tommy's problems.

That night, everyone in the household fell into the first deep sleep that we had experienced in almost eighteen months. The fear that Tommy might do something to us while we slept had kept everyone's "flight or fight" system in overdrive. None of us had been able to sleep peacefully because of our fear of Tommy's violent nature. When I fell into an exhausted sleep, I dreamed for the first time in many months. Dreams that I could remember, at least. Even the baby, Jake, seemed to sleep better that night. I often wondered if he sensed the tension in all of us.

The next morning sunshine beamed through all of the windows in the house, but the silence seemed almost deafening. No fits, no crying, no cursing. Tommy wasn't there. The house was peaceful for the first time since we had gotten custody. The children were actually relaxed.

Seeing the children leave for school with smiles on their faces made me feel better. Bobby and Jake spent a quiet day playing. The feeling inside me seemed so foreign; I hadn't relaxed in so long that I had forgotten what it felt like. I spent those quiet hours enjoying our new little boy.

Mark and I spent the next several nights visiting Tommy at the hospital. He was behaving himself to impress the staff. Unfortunately, his act fooled the doctor. He sent Tommy home a week later with a primary diagnosis of Attention Deficit Hyperactivity Disorder (ADHD). We were in shock. We weren't physicians, but we knew this was not just a hyperactive child. This was a child who was filled with uncontrollable rage. How could a trained professional not have seen through Tommy's act, especially after consulting with Dr. Benson? We felt dejected when we brought Tommy home. The older kids were visibly upset, for the storm cloud was back again.

At our next appointment with Dr. Benson, we expressed our concern that the hospital had only seen Tommy's honeymoon period. She agreed. Together, we decided that if Tommy needed further hospitalization, she would place him under the care of Dr. Felix Ritter. That offered us some reassurance. She respected Dr. Ritter highly and knew he would listen to us and investigate thoroughly before making a final diagnosis of Tommy's problem.

Nothing had changed. Tommy was acting out in a violent manner every day. He was now on an anti-psychotic medication that Dr. Benson had prescribed, but it didn't help. In our hearts, we still were hoping that another hospitalization would not be necessary. However, his time in the hospital and the obvious change in his routine had increased Tommy's rage significantly. Dr. Benson had taught us how to restrain him by using a pillow between the adult and the child and basically laying on top of the child till he calmed down. This sometimes took as long as forty-five minutes. Many days, it was necessary to restrain him more than once. Tommy was now trying harder than ever to injure himself and us. During his fits of rage, he tried to break the windows in his room with his fists and with toys. We had to protect both him and ourselves from his anger. Doing so was fast becoming the entire focus of our lives.

One afternoon, as Mark was restraining Tommy during a particularly violent episode, Tommy bit Mark's hand, breaking the skin. In pain, Mark let go with one hand so that he could inspect the aching wound in the other. Tommy, realizing that Mark was distracted, began thrashing mightily. Seriously disturbed children can have almost super-human strength during their fits of uncontrollable rage. Their strength can even be greater than that of an adult. Mark tried to regain his hold on Tommy, but Tommy used his now freed arms to push himself up off the floor, as if doing a push-up, with Mark still on his back. Mark weighed over two hundred pounds. Tommy lifted his father off the ground like he was nothing. A frigid chill of fear ran through my body. What were we going to do when he got older, bigger and stronger? This raging child was obviously capable of hurting us now. How could we possibly keep him from hurting us then?

The next morning before she left for school, Tommy became angry with Jessica. He was furious that he wasn't allowed to leave for school with her anymore. She started to walk past him, heading for the front door. Without warning, he grabbed her fingers and bit down on them. Her screams of pain ripped through my heart and I raced to see what had happened. As I took Jessica's mangled fingers into my hand to inspect the damage, Tommy stood there with a triumphant grin on his face. That sent a terrifying chill surging through my body. He didn't care! There was absolutely no shred of empathy or remorse inside him! There was no trace of a conscience in Tommy's eyes, only the fire of pure hatred.

The index and middle fingers on Jessie's right hand were bent unnaturally. It was obvious that she needed to go to the emergency room for x-rays. In a panic, trying hard to catch my breath, I called Mark and, once again, he said he'd rush home from work. Meanwhile, I took the baby, Bobby and Jessica to my room and I locked the door, placing a chair against it for added protection. Tommy was screaming and throwing a fit, but I had to protect the other children until Mark got there. Even with the door locked, we were all trembling. It took forty minutes for Mark to get there. Finally I heard him come in the front door. Jessica was still crying and holding her fingers. They had swollen severely in the last hour. I heard Mark telling Tommy that he was pack-ing his clothing to take him back to the hospital. It was ten days before Christmas. We didn't want to put Tommy back in the hospital, but once again, his dangerous behavior had left us with no choice.

I took Jessica, along with Jake and Bobby to the closest urgent care clinic, where her fingers were X-rayed. Her index and middle fingers were broken. They put Jessica's fingers in a splint. Meanwhile, Mark drove Tommy to the hospital for readmission and he raged all the way to the hospital. Worked into an absolute fury, he repeatedly tried to kick the car out of gear while Mark was driving. Somehow, Mark managed to keep Tommy from causing an accident. Covered in a cold sweat and totally exhausted when they finally arrived, Mark physically carried Tommy into the hospital.

When he got back home Mark felt doubly heartbroken. He'd had to hospitalize his son and Jessica had been wounded by the boy. Mark felt guilty about what bringing his two children into the family had done to all of us. He hadn't known that they had serious problems before they came to live with us and it certainly wasn't his fault. Being a parent who took serious responsibility for his children, he felt guilty anyway. I tried to reassure him that we were in this together, that I didn't blame him for any of this. He had done the right thing protecting his kids. I was proud of him for being the kind of man who always tried to do the right thing, even when the right thing ultimately turned out to be so painful.

Dr. Benson had, as she promised, contacted Dr. Ritter and he was now on Tommy's case. I will always be grateful to Dr. Benson for that. Dr. Ritter is a respected psychiatrist who had a gift for seeing the situation as it really was. He wasn't fooled by Tommy's honeymoon behavior. Dr. Benson had given him the complete history. Dr. Ritter called us frequently during the course of the hospitalization, just to keep us informed of what he was doing to help Tommy. His quiet manner and sense of humor made us feel better. He explained that he needed to get Tommy chemically balanced so that he could stop acting out. I prayed every night, hoping with all my heart, that he could.

A new medication, Anafranil, had been added to Tommy's previous medications, Haldol and Clonadine. After a few days, Dr. Ritter said there seemed to be some improvement, and decided to give Tommy a pass to come home for a day. It was a Saturday, Jessica's birthday. Jessica expressed concern that morning that Tommy would do something terrible to ruin her birthday, but I reassured her that Mark and I wouldn't let that happen. After all, Dr. Ritter had said that he was doing much better.

We took Jessica, Bobby and Tommy Christmas shopping that afternoon while Kyle and Jeff watched the baby. Tommy seemed to be doing so well that Mark got his picture taken with his two boys at the store that day. On the way to the car, Mark squeezed my hand. When I turned to look at him, I could see that his heart was filled with hope. I smiled back at him, glad to see him happy. I wanted to believe Tommy was getting better, but experience had taught me to be cautious.

We arrived home in good spirits. Mark and I took some presents we had bought for Jake and the older boys up to our room. Tommy was in his room when Jessica walked in to put away some clean laundry. Once again, a horrible scream pierced a quiet afternoon. Mark, Jeff, Kyle and I raced to Tommy's room. Jessica was up against the wall, her hand cupped over her nose, tears staining her face. Tommy just stood there, as if frozen, with an angry look on his face. He had picked up a yellow Fisher-Price school bus and smashed Jessica's face with it. I screamed in horror, "Take him back, *now!*" Mark sadly led Tommy to the car. You could see that his heart had again been crushed. I spent the rest of the afternoon trying to comfort and apologize to my daughter. Jessica's nose was bruised and swollen from the attack. I asked myself how I could have turned my back on her when Tommy was there, even for a second. How could I have allowed myself to have even the smallest amount of hope? That hope had made me foolish in letting him near Jessica. Tommy had ruined her birthday and I had promised her that we wouldn't let that happen, but it had. You can't go back and undo things that have already happened, but I was determined to try and salvage the evening and give her at least a good birthday dinner. She got her choice of her favorite food, a birthday tradition, and a big cake with ice cream. No one mentioned what had happened that afternoon as we celebrated Jessie's birthday. We didn't talk about it, but you could just tell that it was on everyone's mind. Everyone was tense and overcompensating with small talk. It was like he wasn't there with us, yet he was. The pain he caused just never left.

A couple of days before Christmas, our insurance company notified us our that coverage for Tommy's hospitalization was ending. We would have to take him home for a while and then readmit him if necessary for another short stay. Tommy had to come home again. Many insurance companies treat hospitalizations for mental illnesses like they are fast food restaurants; their goal is to get the patient in, drugged, quiet and then out. Unfortunately, the serious need to actually do something long-term to help the patient often is overlooked. We were learning about the system in a trial by fire. The poor doctors' hands were tied. When the insurance company said it was time to go home, it was time to go home. Dr. Ritter tried to fight for more time, to no avail. The company just didn't seem to care that there was potential danger to family members. After all, the rules were the rules! The short stay was hardly enough to make the slightest dent in Tommy's very serious condition. We all knew it.

We brought Tommy home to a house filled with a dark cloud of dread. All of our fears were quickly confirmed, as his tantrums and violence started up again almost immediately. Dr. Benson resumed seeing him twice a week. We resolved that we would at least try to make it through the holidays without taking him back to the hospital.

Christmas was soon upon us. Despite our fear and consternation, Mark and I tried to make it as special as possible. This was Jake's first Christmas and we were determined not to let Tommy spoil it. The kids woke us up at five that morning and the time we spent opening presents went smoothly. After breakfast, everyone wanted to take their presents to their rooms. Our six-month long conversion of the garage into a bedroom finally had been completed so Jeff and Kyle retreated to the privacy of their new bedroom. Jessica and Bobby took their stash to their room. Mark carried Tommy's toys to his. The house was quiet, too quiet. I turned to Mark, "We'd better go check on Tommy." There he stood in his room, surrounded by his Christmas toys. He had broken practically every one of them and urinated on the rest. Heartsick, we asked him why. He said, "Because I don't want them." His dad and I had taken such care in picking out toys that we thought he would really enjoy, but he had destroyed them already. This was something he would continue to do every Christmas Day thereafter.

I felt totally exhausted, but I ignored the symptoms, telling myself I had to keep going, determined not to quit. Tommy was now threatening to kill everyone in the house and something deep inside me told me that, if given the opportunity, he would. Screamed threats permeated the house for hours. Several times, he tried breaking the window in his room with his balled-up fists. The stench of urine filled his room, because he continued to urinate on the carpet. He scratched and hit us whenever he was given the opportunity. Three days after Christmas, we couldn't take any more. We had to take him back to the hospital.

The trip there was terrifying. Tommy cursed, screamed, hit and kicked furiously. He tried to kick the car out of gear again. I struggled hard to restrain him. I was in the back seat. Tommy was in the front, seated beside Mark. I had to physically wrap my body around his seat from behind it, restraining him to keep him from causing an accident, but Tommy had a physical advantage over me from his adrenaline surge, giving him tremendous strength. He dug his fingernails into my arms, causing me to release his. Then he began clawing and hitting at Mark while Mark tried desperately to maintain control over the car. I desperately struggled to keep him from hurting his father. My muscles were exhausted as I held onto his arms and legs tightly. Tommy dug his fingernails deeply into my arm again, this time drawing blood. People in the cars next to us at the stoplights were staring. My sad eyes met theirs and turned away, embarrassed. They couldn't possibly understand what was going on.

The hospital parking lot was a sight for sore eyes and bodies alike. My arms felt like overstretched rubber bands, as I finally released my grip. Mark picked Tommy up. Tommy fought him at first, but seemed to calm down as we crossed the hospital threshold. During the admission interview, the intake worker to whom we spoke was very kind and understanding as we answered her questions, trying hard to recover from the altercation in the car.

Also present was a home-care social worker, Miss Roberts. She had been sent to meet us by Dr. Ritter. He was planning to have an in-home social worker help us after Tommy's last discharge. Miss Roberts was supposed to have met with us, at home, for the first time that afternoon. I had called her as we left for the hospital and had her meet us there. She was going to help the family deal with Tommy's problems, as well as give us a break when we needed one. Dr. Ritter really cared, not only about Tommy, but the family as well, and we were very grateful for that.

Miss Roberts was tall and beautiful and she had a special kindness in her intelligent and lively brown eyes. Mark and I instantly liked her. Tommy, who lately had abandoned his feigned cuteness when meeting people, gave her a piercing glare, as he aggressively walked up to her. Totally matter-of-factly, he told her, "I want to slit your throat." Miss Roberts took a minute to overcome her shock over what he had just said. She asked him why he would want to do that. He stated, "Because I want to drink your blood!" Everyone in the room seemed to freeze for a moment. Tommy was quickly taken to the upstairs ward where they settled him in, while we filled out the intake paperwork. Miss Roberts listened patiently as we went over the history, yet again. Telling the story over and over was becoming a painful task, but a necessary one. You don't get many choices when it comes to mental illness, every bit of the patient's history is an intricate piece of the puzzle. So you tell the story of the person's life again and again, to all of those trying to help. Sometimes you get so tired of the story that you wish you never had to talk to anyone about it ever again and most times you wish you didn't have to open your mouth in the first place! Always, you just wish the problem would go away and the patient miraculously would get better. This is what we wished for: a miracle.

−chapter nine−

The Diagnosis

This hospitalization was different. Tommy was now telling Dr. Ritter about his angry persona. The boy had named his angry side "Rod." He talked about "Rod" trying to kill him and making him think about violence against other people. Tommy told Dr. Ritter that Rod had held him under the bath water, trying to kill him. He said his angry side was his enemy. Tommy described his darkest homicidal thoughts to his doctor. We had told Dr. Ritter that we often felt that there were different Tommys. There seemed to be a baby, a good Tommy, a goofy Tommy and an evil Tommy. Tommy was put on a new anti-psychotic medication, Resperidal.

One afternoon when Mark was at work, I went to see Tommy alone and we met with a hospital social worker, Dana Franks. We sat in a tiny, closed, almost claustrophobic room that was filled with chairs. I began talking, but within a short while Tommy began to be rude to the social worker. This went on for several minutes. Finally, I got up and walked over to the chair in which he was seated. I leaned forward to talk to him about his bad behavior. Suddenly, Tommy kicked me hard in the chest and sent me reeling backwards. Somehow I got back my balance, clutching my bruised chest with my hand. The social worker immediately called security. Tommy was taken, fighting them all the way, back to his room. He was screaming obscenities which could be heard all the way across the corridor. Dana quickly ushered me to the door, unlocked it and told me, "You have to leave, now!" I burst into tears as the steel door closed and locked behind me.

The incident upset me so badly that I called Sally Benson as soon as I got home, to get her take on what had happened. She reassured me that I had done nothing wrong by trying to correct Tommy's behavior, because I was his acting parent. Dr. Benson called the social worker to get the details. Benson later told me that the social worker said Tommy was the sickest child she had ever seen. Apparently, after I left, Tommy spent the next forty-five minutes cursing, screaming and throwing himself violently around the room and onto the floor. He had bruised himself badly. The staff had to give him an injection of a drug just to calm him down. They now had seen the violence he was capable of. They now had seen the storm that lived inside him. Mark and I felt a torrent of conflicting emotions, sadness that Tommy was so sick and gladness that someone had finally recognized how seriously ill he was.

This hospitalization lasted much longer than the ones that preceded it. During this period I found the older children felt much more at ease with Tommy out of the home. It was such a blessing to see them acting like normal kids. Unfortunately, Tommy was not faring as well. He was beginning to have a reaction to the new drug he'd been given. He had developed tardive dyskinesia, a movement disorder associated with side effects from anti-psychotic medicines. His tongue continually pushed into his cheek, sliding across his cheek and finally out of his mouth. The medication had to be stopped because of this reaction. Dr. Ritter also took him off Prozac. However, there was one light in this tunnel. Dr. Ritter had made a final diagnosis. We would at last know what was wrong with Tommy. The diagnosis was schizophrenia, disorganized type. Tommy was very young to be diagnosed with this disease. However, Dr. Ritter felt he was correct, especially because of Tommy's reaction to antidepressants. The theory is that antidepressants will make a schizophrenic who's prone to violence more violent. Tommy's disorganized mental state and psychotic thinking fit into the diagnosis criteria. At last, we had something concrete to work with. We had a name for the primary problem. But still on top of the primary diagnosis of schizophrenia was the PTSD that Tommy suffered. Dr. Ritter had also identified that Tommy had both suicidal and homicidal thoughts. Having a diagnosis made us feel better, in the sense that maybe there were drugs that could help Tommy. It didn't, however, alleviate our fears. He was suffering from serious mental illness.

It wasn't too long after the diagnosis that our insurance company again told us our hospital coverage was ending. Tommy had to come home. However, Tommy was still very angry and violent towards family members and continued to attack the hospital staff. Still we knew it did no good to point this out to our insurance company and Mark and I were so exhausted from the back-to-back, non-productive hospitalizations that we consciously decided we wouldn't send him back again. We were frustrated that the hospitalizations were so short that little progress was made and that he kept coming home on new medications which only worked for a brief period and then would be overridden by his illness. Once home, Tommy filled our days with tantrums. Trying to restrain him, we used cold showers, a method that had been suggested by the hospital, even though we hated giving them to him. To us, this method, and even the very act of restraining him, felt barbaric. The cold water was supposed to snap him back to reality. But the way Tommy fought us, we all ended up getting a cold shower along with him. However, the cold water would often make him calm down for an hour or so. Nevertheless, our guilty feelings over having to use these severe methods to calm a violent child were overwhelming.

Miss Jones had recommended that we turn the doorknob on Tommy's room around, locking him in during the night. This was the only way we could be safe while sleeping. She recognized that we were in serious danger from Tommy. We were afraid it might be illegal. She assured us that the Department of Social Services would agree that it was necessary in this particular situation. We had an obligation to protect the other children from danger in their home. Miss Jones told us the DSS would understand that. We also put an alarm on the door, to warn us if Tommy broke the door lock and opened the door. We didn't like locking him in at night, but we did feel more secure knowing he was in his room. We knew by this time we had to do it to survive. We didn't have a choice anymore.

Dr. Benson was doing all that she could for Tommy as an outpatient and we were trying everything we knew to keep him calm. Nevertheless, our family perpetually walked on eggshells. Normalcy for us was a day filled with Tommy's threats and fits. I could barely remember what life had been like before he came to live with us. I was afraid if I thought about it too much, I would want to leave and I loved Mark too much to bear the thought.

The school staff acted glad when Tommy returned. However, the scratching tic we had told the school about, a side effect of his medication, had worsened. Tommy scratched his arms until he drew blood. We had told his teacher about this, but for some reason she now decided that Tommy had, of all things, scabies. Scabies are mites that live in an area of the body and dig noticeable furrows under the skin, causing intense itching. Having looked up scabies in a medical book and seen a picture, I knew this wasn't scabies. The furrows leave long white lines under the skin. An unclean, unsanitary, living environment usually causes scabies and a social stigma is often attached.

Tommy was taken to the nurse's office where his arms were bandaged. Jessica was pulled out of class, unaware of the reason why, and was sent to the school nurse where her arms were searched for signs of scabies. She felt totally humiliated. The nurse called and told me to pick both children up immediately. She told me to take Jessica and Tommy for an examination by a doctor. They would not be allowed to return to school without a physician's note stating that they did not have scabies. Tommy already had an appointment with Dr. Benson that afternoon. I was visibly upset when I took him to see her. Jessica attended the appointment as well.

Dr. Benson took one look at Tommy's arms and said it was the tic she had seen during his previous appointments that caused Tommy to scratch ferociously. She wrote the school a note which explained that this break-out was yet another one of Tommy's motor tics and definitely *not* scabies!

After this Tommy had several unusually bad days in a row. He was totally inconsolable, seeming very out of touch with reality. The pressure cooker that was building inside him finally exploded late one afternoon.

Reeling from an all-day tantrum, we put him in the kitchen for a time out. I was trying to cook dinner, but it was painfully obvious that I needed to keep an eye on him because of the severity of his recent episodes. As Tommy screamed in the time-out chair, Mark and I pleaded with him to tell us what was wrong. He seemed to be making no real sense. Desperately trying to calm him down, we told him that we would love him no matter what. Over and over, we reassured him that nothing he told us would ever, *ever*, make us stop loving him. Finally, sobbing so hard it shook his small body, he began to tell us something we were horrified to hear. With a lost and distant look in his eyes, he began describing his mother sucking on his penis. We were totally floored by this revelation, but Tommy grew eerily calm after telling us the dark memories that were causing him so much pain.

Mark and I both simultaneously put our arms around him, telling him that we loved him. Tears flowed from both our eyes and we all held each other tightly. Without hesitation, I told my sobbing stepson, "You never have to worry that I would touch you that way." I felt nausea welling up in me as I left the kitchen. My mind just couldn't fathom a mother molesting her own child. Children were to be loved, not abused. The very thought sickened me to the core of my being.

Shaking all over, I immediately called Dr. Benson to tell her about Tommy's newest horrible revelation. She had always told us that the more he trusted us over time, the more he would reveal. Now he had told us what had to be the ultimate betrayal of a child. How would he ever trust anyone again? I now understood why Tommy seemed to hate women. The one person that should have been protecting him had betrayed him beyond all reason. This made me furiously angry. That anger strengthened my resolve to fight that much harder to help the boys. The petrified look on Tommy's face was stamped on my memory. I knew I would never, ever, forget it.

The stress I was under was so unrelenting that I was feeling like a frayed piece of cotton fabric. I felt like I was unraveling further with each new issue. Financially, we were getting deeper in debt because of the boys' problems. Still, Mark and I resolved to keep trying. There was never any question that it was the right thing to do.

I had asked the school to evaluate the state of Tommy's emotional disturbance. It was essential that his problems be properly classified within the school system so he could get the services he needed and to protect the other students at the school. I felt the school officials weren't listening and they put off my request. I felt angry especially in light of the fact that changing him to a half-day program had precipitated the rage which sent him to the mental hospital for the first time. Desperate for help, I called the Rights for Virginians with Disabilities advocate. Afterward, the school reluctantly conceded to re-evaluate Tommy.

A few days later school officials noticed Tommy had a small brown bruise on his cheek. It came from Jessica's first effort at self-defense. It was the size of a dime. He had hit her the week before and she had finally defended herself. We were trying to see if natural consequences for his behavior helped him to stop his attacks. It was hoped that if Jessica defended herself once, he would not attack her again. Dr. Benson thought it was at least worth a try. Jessica hadn't wanted to hit him back when he hit her in the face, but she did as she was instructed and returned his punch. He also had a small paperclip sized bruise on his ear from his constant pinching of his ear. It was another one of his nervous tics. He would pinch himself hard in various places, all over his body, until he bruised himself; occasionally he even pinched off large pieces of skin, drawing his own blood. It was a form of self-mutilating behavior.

The home social worker who had replaced Miss Jones knew of Tommy's long history of self-inflicted injuries and hadn't even questioned the minor bruises. She was there the afternoon when Jessica and Jeff came home from school. They both were visibly upset. Two social workers from the Department of Social Services had removed them from class and questioned them about how I disciplined Tommy.

The kids had told them all about how Tommy was hurting himself and assaulting the family continually. Jessica explained that she had caused the bruise on his cheek in self-defense. Both children were intensely questioned at their respective schools and their stories were found to be identical. They gave Jessica a business card and asked that I call them. The caseworker on the phone was very nice. She reassured me that she already knew the claims were not justified. She had talked with Tommy that afternoon, duly noting his being out of touch with reality. Jeff and Jessica had separately told them identical stories about what Tommy was doing to the family. She told me that a teacher at Tommy's school had called their office. According to the law, the social worker had to come to the home to meet me and investigate. That was just fine with me!

She reassured me that after talking to Dr. Benson and the hospital, the incident would be over. His teachers had grilled Tommy, over and over, who had said his "mommy" hurt him. Tommy had told them the truth. Well, of course, his mommy hurt him, just not his "Beth mommy," as he called me. With an apology, the social worker left after commending me for doing a good job trying to help Tommy. That offered some consolation for the intense hurt and humiliation of being falsely accused of child abuse.

A week later, I got a letter stating that I was innocent of the charges and that I had the right to sue the person making the false claim. A copy of the letter was also sent to the school personnel who had made the accusation. If I petitioned the court, they would have to give me the exact names of the people who actually made the accusations. That was not my aim; my goal was to get help for Tommy. At last one good thing now had happened. The school had to face the fact that Tommy was seriously mentally ill.

My mother had decided to sell her house in North Carolina and move to Virginia. We were trying to decide what the living arrangements should be. One of our ideas was to build an addition on to our existing house for Mom; another was to buy a new and larger house altogether. We all went into this arrangement with excitement. Mom was always great with the kids and a big help around the house. Sometimes, she worked a little too hard, but I loved her for her enthusiasm and zest for life. She had a strong work ethic, excelling in her jobs since Dad had left her. I admired her strength and determination to always keep going, no matter what.

Mom had the same positive "I can fix this" attitude toward Tommy that I had in the beginning. However, it didn't take long for her to see that she couldn't fix him either. No amount of attention would take this child's rage away. Nothing could even knock it down a single notch.

Though my mother tried so hard to reach Tommy, each time she thought she had made a breakthrough, Tommy did something awful. Mom was very worried about what his behavior was doing to our family, especially to me. She couldn't stand seeing me hurting. I had learned everything about a mother's love from her. I was still learning from her each day as I watched her struggle to help Tommy. She just wouldn't give up. I guess that's where I got my determination to never give up on my stepson. Seeing her frustrated by Tommy just broke my heart. Now she was suffering because of him as well.

With our increased need to support each other as we cared for the children and sought aid for Tommy, Mark made the decision to get out of the Navy the following September. Looking toward a new beginning gave us something to hope for and mercifully distracted us from our nightmare home life with Tommy. Mark began looking for jobs in the local area while he was finishing up his studies at the technical college in the field of computer programming.

A short while after Mark decided to leave the Navy his parents came down for a visit. They enjoyed meeting Mom and all seemed to be going well. It was so good to see them with no court appearance in the wings. Just a visit, a simple normal visit to their grandchildren and son.

Mark needed to talk to his parents alone about his impending career change. There was an air show at the Navy base, so I bravely decided to take Tommy, Bobby, Jessica and Kyle. I wasn't usually coura- geous enough to take Tommy anywhere by myself at that point, because of his behavior, but I wanted to give Mark time alone with his folks. Tommy threw a tantrum before we left, because he didn't want to wear his socks. It was a hot day and his feet always sweated a lot. While I understood his complaint, I insisted that he wear them to prevent his getting blisters from his new shoes. He calmed down quickly after Mark backed me up.

We found a good parking space on the base and unloaded the kids from the car. Jessica picked up Bobby, who just couldn't walk that far. It was a long walk to the air show from the parking lot. I was so proud of my daughter. She had a mothering instinct well beyond her years, as well as a genuine heart of gold. She was always so good to Tommy and Bobby. Even when Tommy was mean to her, she was still kind to him. Suddenly, as we were walking Tommy crossed directly in front of me and kicked Jessica's legs out from under her. With nothing to brace her- self on, she fell, with Bobby in her arms, face first onto the rough sur- face of the tarmac. It looked like it all happened in slow motion as I watched them hit the hot asphalt. Instantly, Kyle and I reached down to pick them up. Blood was already flowing from their wounded faces, elbows and knees. Bobby was screaming; Jessica was in tears. Tommy just stood there. "Why did you do this?" There was no emotion in his voice when he said, "Because I wanted to."

Kyle carried Bobby and I helped Jessica back to the car. Using the baby wipes in my purse I carried in my purse, I applied them to the bleeding wounds. Anger swelled up inside me. My attempt at doing something good for Mark had been foiled by Tommy. I felt frustrated and hurt. Tears fell from my eyes all the way home.

Mark came rushing to the car when he heard us. Bobby was crying his eyes out. I was thanking God that I had decided to leave the baby at home that afternoon. If he had fallen to the pavement as hard as Bobby had, our little one would have been hurt badly. Mom rushed to help Jessica and Bobby tend their wounds.

Mark's mom became agitated. First, she commented Jessica wasn't watching where she was going. Then she said that I shouldn't have made Tommy wear his socks if he didn't want to, insinuating that this incident wouldn't have happened had I let the child have his way. Perry sounded like she was essentially blaming me for what happened. Her words cut like a knife to my heart. For the next hour, I cooked dinner in silence. Mark had punished Tommy but, as usual, he didn't even seem to care. When dinner was ready, I dropped the dishtowel I was twisting into knots and announced that I was going shopping with Jessica. Everyone looked totally surprised as Jessica and I left the house while they sat down to dinner. However, I needed to get my emotions under control, to help my daughter and to try to understand where Mark's mother was coming from. Mom had picked up on the same hurtful remarks from Perry, and made no attempt to stop me. Normally, she would have freaked out over my apparent rudeness to company but, deep inside, I felt like she was proud of me for taking a stand.

As I cooled down I started to think she had spoken this way probably because it was too hard for Perry to accept that Tommy was mentally ill. It was easier to assume it was my or Jessica's fault. We were scapegoats for Tommy's attack. Granted, I had made him wear socks when he didn't want to. Isn't that what a mother is supposed to do? Make appropriate decisions for their child? And Jessica was certainly blameless.

Years down the road, I would realize that Perry's own guilt over not recognizing the abuse that Tommy and Bobby had suffered while living in Maine had been haunting her. I have come to understand that at times, you just can't see what is going on until hindsight makes it apparent. That's just the way reality is sometimes. Perry and Bob had nothing to feel guilty about. They had done their best for the boys, always.

Waiting until Mark's parents departed, we then put Tommy back in the expert care of Dr. Ritter. He put Tommy in the hospital, trying to stabilize him again. Within two weeks, we got a letter in the mail stating that Tommy had gone over the forty-five day maximum hospital stay limit for the year. They would not pay for the last few days he had already spent in the hospital. It would cost us roughly a thousand dollars a day. We were numb from shock. We explained to Dr. Ritter that there was no way we could afford this kind of money. Dr. Ritter told us he would not charge us for his services and would help us transfer Tommy to the state mental hospital, two hours away.

– c h a p t e r   t e n –

Crazy Mentality

Mark drove Tommy to the state hospital on the first of June. Again, he had to go through the tedious intake process. Emotionally and physically drained, Mark came home in a very solemn mood. All he said to me was that Ted Carter, a young psychology resident, had been assigned to Tommy's case. This concerned us because we knew by this time that schizophrenia is a disease of the brain which requires medication. A psychiatrist, Dr. Wayne, was overseeing the work of Dr. Carter.

Dr. Carter decided right away that Dr. Ritter's diagnosis had to be wrong. Tommy was again on a honeymoon period and behaving well. Dr. Carter acknowledged that Tommy obviously had brain damage, but he said he didn't think Tommy was schizophrenic. Despite Dr. Ritter's expert diagnosis, at the recommendation of the psychology resident Tommy was taken off all his medications.

Mark and I had a meeting with Dr. Carter about two weeks after Tommy's admission. Mark's parents had come to see us. They visited with Tommy while we met with Dr. Carter. While I was telling him all that we had gone through with Tommy, I sensed a cold and disinterested attitude. I would later find out from Dr. Benson that, in Dr. Carter's opinion, I was to blame for Tommy's bad behavior, that I was putting him in the hospital because I wanted to get rid of the child. As he put it, "I had my own agenda." What possible reason could I have for going to such dramatic lengths to get Tommy out of the house? If I had just wanted to get rid of him, we could have sent him back to his mother at any time and life would have been much easier on the entire family. The prejudicial stereotype of an unloving stepmother was very hurtful when I found out that Dr. Carter had this bad opinion of me. I had spent the last two years trying to help this child. Helping this child had, in fact, taken over my life.

I just didn't understand how Dr. Carter couldn't see what Dr. Benson and Dr. Ritter had both seen and diagnosed. They were both highly respected psychiatrists with decades more experience and training than Dr. Carter. This naïve young resident totally missed the mark. Was it so hard for him to believe that a stepmother could care for her stepson as much as I did? I thought it was such a shame that he couldn't come to my home to just observe Tommy and the way he treated us, as well as to witness firsthand the unending efforts we made to love and nourish him.

Dr. Benson did all that she could professionally to make Dr. Carter realize the depth of Tommy's illness. She talked to him several times and faxed over sixty pages of her records to him. He coldly dismissed her professional opinion as completely invalid. Mark and I were deeply concerned about Tommy's care. We met with Dr. Benson to express our concerns. With her usual tact and sympathetic manner, she explained to us that sometimes you come up against doctors like this.

A few days later, Mark and I had a team meeting with Dr. Carter, Dr. Wayne and several others who were working with Tommy. During the meeting I summoned up my courage and pointed out that I still agreed with Dr. Ritter's diagnosis of schizophrenia and made a point of telling them about Tommy's increasing incidences of violence in the presence of antidepressant medication.

Dr. Carter was livid at my insinuation that his diagnosis was incorrect. He had decided that Tommy had cerebral palsy and was not mentally ill. When Dr. Wayne agreed with me, he became outraged and when the committee agreed that Tommy needed residential care for his mental illness, Dr. Carter stormed out of the meeting.

Jessica had come with us, wanting to see Tommy. She was waiting outside the room for us, and after the meeting, we all went to visit him. Tommy, watching television, ignored us. However, when I stepped over to privately chat with Mark, Tommy made his move. He walked up to Jessica and whispered, "I'm gonna kill you, you fucking bitch!" She quietly came up to me, telling me what had just happened. I reported the threat to the staff. Tommy was taken to the time-out room where he began venting the rage he had pent up for weeks. He threw himself violently against the walls of the padded room and threw his shoes at the staff as they tried to calm him. I requested that they summon Dr. Wayne so that he could observe Tommy.

Dr. Wayne was apparently meeting with the other people that had attended our meeting. Dr. Carter was paged instead. Obviously still reeling from the meeting, he stormed onto the ward. He snatched Tommy up, practically dragging the screaming child with him into Tommy's room, slamming the door behind him. Tommy began screaming even more hysterically.

A short while later Dr. Carter came out of Tommy's room looking very angry. "Leave immediately," he said. It must have been easier for him to believe that we had provoked Tommy, than to accept the fact that he had misdiagnosed him. Mark and I were crushed as we turned and with Jessica left the ward as requested.

Occasionally, you run into people like Dr. Carter when you have a mentally ill family member. Experience has taught me that you have to take their opinions with a grain of salt and seek the counsel and aid of someone more willing to look at the whole picture. You know in your heart what the truth is and eventually it always comes out. It hurts when you get criticized and wrongly blamed for the problems of a mentally ill loved one, but you just have to stay focused and keep going. It's incredibly hard, but you just have to let the hurt go. Wallowing won't help the mentally ill family member or yourself, for that matter.

After much discussion with Dr. Benson, Mark and I decided to pull Tommy out of the hospital. Dr. Carter offered no objection. On the weekend of the Fourth of July, we had Tommy discharged. To us it was better to have to put up with Tommy's violence, than to have him wrongly diagnosed and incorrectly treated. We put Tommy back under Dr. Benson's care. She immediately put Tommy back on medication.

However, our finances were at the breaking point. After searching for work all over our vicinity, Mark began to look in other states. Finally, he found a job and a reasonably priced large seven-bedroom home on the outskirts of a small town in Alabama. We moved and put the children in new schools. After a peaceful lull which saw a little improvement in Tommy's behavior, the head of Mark's company decided to close the office. Mark had to find a new job, which, being proactive, he did, only this time it was in North Carolina. Until we were able to sell the house, he came home only on weekends. And, on one of his visits, to our surprise, I became pregnant—with twins.

—chapter eleven—

Out of the Lull

The move to North Carolina was difficult. The driveway of our new house was on a 45-degree incline, significantly complicating the task of carrying in the extremely large load of heavy furniture. The long drive there and back, along with the daunting physical task of moving, had worn Mark, Jeff and Kyle out, but they never complained. With Kyle remaining in North Carolina, Mark and Jeff drove back for Jessica, Jake, Tommy, Bobby and me.

When we stopped to eat lunch, I walked over to the car Jeff was driving and looked in on Tommy. Peering through the car window, I watched Tommy had pulled his penis out of his shorts and masturbate furiously. It was just the beginning of what was to come.

After we moved there was no doubt Tommy was getting worse. The change in his routine made him act out more violently. Once again, I was afraid for my other children and myself. Because of Tommy's past history, I insisted that Mark put an alarm and lock on Tommy's bedroom door. Making sure we were going to be safe at night was more important than anything else that had to be done in the new home.

The Monday after we arrived in North Carolina, I took Tommy and

Bobby to register for school, bringing Jake with me. Nervous with anticipation, I wasn't sure what I should tell them. I didn't want to panic the
school over Tommy's behavior, but I felt I had to warn them, especially
about keeping him away from sharp objects, for the sake of the other
students. The danger we lived through at home made me feel I had a
responsibility to try and help the teachers protect other students from
him.

The principal seemed responsive to everything I told her, at first.
When I finished, she said that they would need to evaluate Tommy and
Bobby, by their school's standards and form their own opinion regarding the boys. *Here we go again*, I thought to myself. No one ever seemed
to really pay attention to Tommy's record or history of violence. Once
again, I felt like the schools were blowing me off.

I also knew that during Tommy's honeymoon period, he could be
overly compliant and very polite. This always gave the school the opinion that we were exaggerating what he was really like. Past experience
had taught us to expect this reaction, and Tommy's eventual explosion
always came like clockwork. Nevertheless, with all we'd experienced,
having the school doubt what we were telling them always caused us
much frustration. Fortunately, it never took very long for them to see
exactly what we were talking about.

My pregnancy was weighing heavily on my body. My belly was
growing rapidly and I looked nine months pregnant by my fifth month.

Soon Tommy's threats were growing more sinister. My stepson
often screamed through the door of his room that he wanted to murder
us all. Yelling loudly, he told us just how he planned to do it. The stress
of dealing with Tommy was very difficult. We all lived with constant
fear.

Yet I still felt compassion for Tommy. He had no control over the
circumstances that made him the way he was. Nevertheless, his hatred
sent waves of fear all through me. As hard as I tried to love him, and as
hard as Jessica tried as well, he still hated us because we were born
female, targeting us incessantly with his plethora of rage in a futile
attempt to punish his mother. Taking care of Tommy daily was a risk to
my pregnancy, because he was growing more out of control.

He told his new psychologist that the three things he wanted most
were "a leprechaun that he could knock the living daylights out of,

twins and a sister who is nice to me and doesn't hit me." Tommy was clearly dangerous and delusional.

We were living a nightmare and Mark and I didn't know how to get our family out of it. Everyone's desire to help Tommy was so strong, but we didn't know what to do. We had tried everything! Nothing, not drugs, not therapy, not behavior modification, not discipline, not structure and not love, nothing, had ever made even a dent in Tommy's condition. Having no success, we felt totally helpless and, frankly, we were.

A beautiful miracle was growing inside of me and I was thrilled, but I was also very frightened. If Tommy had been a grown man, I would have left him in a heartbeat. Because he was a child, I felt I had no choice but to try and stick it out. You can divorce an abusive husband, but you can't leave a mentally ill child. I felt caught between protecting the other children and helping Tommy. My life was a tug of war. I often envisioned myself as a batch of taffy on a taffy-pulling machine—stretched to the limits, twisted around, pulled in another direction, stretched out again, in a seemingly never-ending cycle. Our entire family was suffering because of the illness of one member. His intense needs overshadowed the needs of everyone else. It was as if this eight-year-old boy was in control of our lives and we were helpless to stop his reign of terror.

Having one baby is scary enough, but the possibility of complications with twins was even greater. My pregnancy with Jacob had been fraught with problems. The older children now pitched in to allow me to rest when I could. Having these babies became a family project. The camaraderie was unbelievable. Nevertheless, my body was growing weary as the babies grew and grew. Because of my prolapsed uterus, I carried them extremely low. Walking was becoming increasingly difficult. Filled with stress, I wasn't gaining as much weight as I should. At night, I prayed that I could hold these precious angels inside me, at least long enough for them to let their lungs mature.

At first we didn't want to know the babies' genders, but as the ultrasound progressed, we changed our minds. Jessica was hoping for a sister. Her joy was infectious when we called to tell her that she was getting two new baby sisters. She started squealing with happiness so loudly that Mark had to hold the cell phone away from his ear. A part of me was elated that the babies were girls; a part of me was terrified because of Tommy's hatred of females. Having five boys already, Mark and I had wanted daughters so badly. With Tommy in the home, this cause for celebration was more a call to new fear.

As the school year wound down in late May, I counted the days in anticipation. Having my older kids home to help me in my last trimester of pregnancy would be so wonderful.

The day school let out for vacation was a happy one for me. Finally, the time I looked forward to every year had arrived. Spending time with my children was one of my greatest joys. But having Tommy home for the summer would, I feared, be hell. Yet another change in his routine would send him spiraling further downward.

As much as I would have loved to make new friends in the neighborhood, I didn't dare. I felt I just couldn't bear explaining Tommy's problems to strangers, much less to people who might gossip. I didn't want anyone to know about our private heartbreak that we couldn't help this child become emotionally well. Many of the women in the neighborhood approached me during the first few months in our new home, asking me to their homes or to join them in some activity. However, I knew most of them had small children that Tommy might hurt if they were around him. I just couldn't let something like that happen. I knew better than to let Tommy play with other children. My overwhelming sense of responsibility kept me vigilant in making sure that he didn't hurt anyone.

A week before school ended, Tommy's behavior began worsening. He was furious about school ending. His death threats were becoming more frequent and vicious. He was regularly hosing down his room in urine. I felt exhausted, as I spent a lot of time cleaning his carpet and washing his toys and bed sheets over and over. My doctors advised that I take bed rest, an impossibility because of the demands of taking care of Tommy. There were many times when I had to sit on him to keep him from hurting himself or me. It was the only way to break the spell he seemed to be under. Cold showers seemed to be totally ineffective at this point.

My mother was extremely worried about the twins I was carrying when I told her about having to restrain Tommy. Mark had to work every day and there was no one else to keep him from hurting himself and others, only me. As a parent, I couldn't, wouldn't dump my burden on my older kids. I didn't like restraining Tommy; it went against all of the images of mothering I had ever imagined, but I was left with absolutely no choice in the matter. Better me holding him down than him putting his fist through another window.

On the first of July, Mark's parents came to visit us for the first time since we had moved to Alabama and then to North Carolina. Jessica and I had long since forgiven them for the incident in Virginia, where they blamed us for Tommy's behavior. Their new level of understanding had drawn them to us and they now knew Tommy had very real problems. We were glad they had come to visit.

Mark's mom's health had been steadily declining, but she was a fighter. The week before their trip, Perry had been in the hospital with pneumonia. Almost as soon as she was released, Perry said nothing was going to stop her from seeing her grandkids! Tommy began baby talking when he saw his grandparents. Seeing them sent immediate fear running through him and he thought that they were here to take him back to Maine. Mark and I did our best to reassure him that he wouldn't be going back to Maine.

Tommy drew two very disturbing pictures for his grandmother. One was of a black house that he said had a wall of blood that trapped all of the people inside. The wall of blood was engulfing the house from the outside. The other picture was of a mental hospital that he told us he lived in, along with his Gayle mommy. Resembling something out of a horror movie, it was a large building, full of windows, with multi-colored, squiggly lines seeming to burst forth from it. Perry admitted to me that this was the first time she had realized how disturbed he really was. Her eyes were finally open. I know it broke her heart, but she finally faced the painful truth. Tommy had more than problems; Tommy was very sick!

Tommy seemed to be relieved when his grandparents left without taking him back to Maine with them. The disruption of their visit, however, caused his outbursts to escalate to a new level. We heard him in his room, talking to people who weren't there. We knew he had both visual and auditory hallucinations from time to time, but now he seemed to be having actual full-blown conversations with an evil entity. We could hear him talking to the devil. He was saying, "But I love you devil," as if he was trying to convince the devil that he did indeed love him. This scared me to death. No one in the house had ever mentioned the devil to Tommy before. I had told the children about a kind and forgiving God. Scaring little kids by talking of the devil was something I was totally against. Somehow, Tommy had found out about the devil all by himself. His newfound friend terrified us all.

It felt like my family was descending into hell along with Tommy. We began overhearing Tommy threatening to kill the babies. He wanted to strangle our unborn daughters. My promise to help my husband raise his children was becoming a curse on everyone I loved and wanted to protect. At night, the guilt I felt over the suffering of the other children because of Tommy would not leave me.

Two weeks after Bob and Perry left to go home, I was fixing Tommy's favorite hot dogs for dinner. That night, however, he started complaining loudly about not wanting them. Exhausted, I told him, "You need to eat what is on your plate." He started screaming.

After dinner he began vomiting, as he seemed to do at will, all over his plate. Kyle and Jessica jumped back from the table in horror. He just smiled, stood up and vomited more. As I ordered him to go to his room, he began screaming curses. Refusing to go, Tommy flailed his arms at me. There was no choice at this point but to wrap my arms around him to try to restrain the screaming child so that I could get him back to his room. Tommy fought me hard until he was able to turn around facing me. He then proceeded to vomit all over the front of my maternity dress. Waves of my own nausea caused me to let go of him. Trying to contain my own emotions, I ordered Tommy into the bathroom. Quickly, I ran in behind him, just in time to reach the toilet. As I stood there vomiting, Tommy grinned, as if proud of what he had done.

Recovered enough to stand up again, I gave Tommy a shower, brushed his teeth and gave him some water. He quietly went to his room. Heading for a shower of my own, tears welled up inside of me. Once in the shower, a torrent of tears flowed from my eyes, my body shaking. Praying out loud, I begged God, "Please help us get through this. How much more can we possibly take?"

Kyle and Jessica quietly began cleaning up the living room carpet and the table. They did so without complaint. Their silence spoke volumes of their hurt. Opening the bedroom door to check on Tommy, I saw he had vomited the water all over the carpet in his room. He stood next to the door smiling at me. Cold chills ran down my spine. I was afraid of this child, afraid in my own home!

In the days that followed, his death threats became progressively worse. Jessica was still his primary target. Tommy kept calling her a "fucking bitch" and a "whore" every chance he got. At dinner now, he would threaten to kill her, often menacing her with a fork. Most of the time at dinner the tension was so thick that Mark and I were too upset to even eat. Conversation had become virtually impossible; dinner ended almost every night with Tommy having to be removed from the table and sent to his room. Eventually, we tried seating Tommy at an end table behind his father, with his back turned to us. Defiant, he still made his threats. Nothing ever seemed to stop him when he was obsessed with doing something. Whenever an impulse struck him, he acted on it. As a last resort, for the sake of the other children, as well as for our sanity, we finally began serving him his dinner in his room.

Tommy was now including Jake in his death threats. He talked about wanting to beat Jacob to death. He was always in his room, sitting on his bed, talking to someone who didn't exist, about killing Jake and Jessica.

School started in early August. The six hours Tommy spent at school at least gave me a physical break from him, but certainly not an emotional one. While he was gone, all I could do was think about what he might be doing at school and what he would do when he came home.

On the 13th of August, Tommy attacked my unborn babies. As he walked past me in the hallway, headed from the bathroom to his bedroom, he suddenly stopped and looked right at me with his angry face. Without warning, he elbowed me very hard in the stomach. Doubling over in pain, I clutched my belly as I fell back against the wall. Tommy just looked at me with pure hatred in his eyes and it took me a few seconds to get my bearings back. Pulling myself back up, still reeling from the painful blow, I herded him quickly into his room. Panic ripped through me, as I rubbed my belly, desperate to stimulate movement in each baby. Tears streamed from my eyes as I waited for any sign that they were unharmed. A few minutes later I felt both babies moving. I was flooded with tearful emotion. They had to be okay. I knew, via the ultrasound, that the babies' placentas were not in the location where he'd hit me, and thanked God for that. Tommy's action had made it painfully apparent that he hated these babies. They were unborn but already new targets.

I feared what Tommy might do when Mark and I were at the hospital having the babies. Tommy's rage left me trembling with fear every time I had to leave home so that I could keep my doctor appointments. Knowing that I would soon have to leave home for a few days to give birth was painfully frightening. Mark was feeling the same anxiety.

When my first contraction hit, I was home alone with the children. There was no pain, but a lot of pressure. My body felt like it was on autopilot, ready to push the babies out of my womb at any minute. Survival instinct quickly overcame fear and I told Jeff to call an ambulance. The poor kid's voice was cracking as he spoke to the 911 dispatcher, but he did a good job of telling them what the problem was and where we lived. They were based just down the road from us and, to our complete surprise, were there within two minutes of Jeff hanging up the phone.

An eerie sense of calm washed over me like a shower of gentle raindrops. I felt peaceful, even though I had an overwhelming sense that my babies were in trouble. Oddly, something kept telling me that everything was going to turn out fine. I've always thought that was a final loving gift from my beloved grandmother. Grandma had died a month before. The last thing she had written to me was, "I wish I could be there to help you with the twins." Knowing my grandmother's time was near, my dad had given her a special message from me a week or so before she passed on. The message was, "I'll be waiting for you to come help me with the babies and watch over us." Dad said she seemed to understand exactly what I meant. Now, with my babies' birth imminent, I could feel her unearthly presence with me. Transcending the boundaries of death, she was there with me in my greatest time of need. Feelings of gentle warmth surrounded me, making the emergency at hand seem surreal. My beloved grandmother's heavenly comfort cushioned me from my fear. It was her gift of love for me and the great-grandchildren she had so longed to see. At a time when I had every right to feel terrified, I found myself feeling safe and inexplicably calm.

With the help of an emergency Caesarian section, the babies arrived. Mark held Kristen for several minutes, his face glowing as only the face of a new father could. All of my babies before her had been big. Never before had I seen an infant so tiny. Her little face was that of an angel. Staring at her, I could scarcely believe we had actually brought forth these two beautiful miracles. They brought Megan over for us to look at. Even though they were fraternal twins, they looked exactly like one another. Soon, they would be taking Megan to the Special Care Nursery. Kristen would be going to the regular nursery. Separating my babies was upsetting to me. They had been together since the day they were conceived and now they were parted on the day they came into the world. I understood why, but I was still unhappy about the necessary separation.

Mark accompanied me to recovery, where I developed the shakes badly. This was a side effect of the morphine they had given me during my surgery. My teeth were chattering so much that I could barely talk, but I was still able to convey to Mark that I wanted him to call home. Even after a caesarian, my mind was still full of frightening thoughts about what Tommy might be doing, knowing that we weren't home.

Watching from his bedroom window, he had seen me taken away in the ambulance. In fact, when Mark called, he was throwing another tantrum. Kyle and Jessica downplayed his behavior to make Mark feel better about staying with me. They knew how much I needed him.

After an hour had passed, the shaking subsided, I was taken to a private room, very weak and sore. Mark was allowed to spend the night. I had mistakenly assumed that they would at least bring Kristen to see me, since she was in the regular nursery. As time passed, we wondered where she was.

Soon, the neonatal specialist, a kind, soft-spoken man, showed up and announced that he was the babies' doctor and was there to tell me about their conditions. Kristen, the smaller twin, had suddenly developed breathing problems. She had been moved to the special care nursery with her sister. Megan was fairly stable. The doctor reassured us that he would keep us informed of any changes. His compassion and confidence made me have complete trust in him. Mark and I were both understandably worried, but knew the babies were in the best neonatal nursery in the area. The nurses told me they would let me go to the nursery twelve hours after surgery. That would mean 4:30 A.M., and I held them to their promise.

As I was wheeled toward the nursery, I began to feel all shaky inside, dreading what I might see. After washing my hands, I was wheeled over to Megan's small plastic bassinet. There lay a tiny, red-skinned baby with a thick patch of dark hair, just like her daddy's. Her face looked healthy, but her body was very scrawny. I stroked her hair, and tears began to well up in my eyes. Then I was wheeled over to see Kristen. Her legs and arms were even smaller than Megan's. Her face was not as plump and healthy looking as her big sister. Her hair was dark, like her sister's, but she had less of it. An oxygen tube was in her nose to help her breathe. Overhead, monitors beeped softly with every beat of my babies' hearts. They were comforting, because I knew they would immediately let the nurses know if there were a problem. They were also disturbing, as I knew they were there only because there might be a problem.

My arms ached to hold my infants, to breast feed them so we could bond. It didn't seem natural, not being able to cuddle them. I gently stroked Kristen's hair, afraid to touch her body because of all the wires. I told each baby that I loved her and was taken back to my room. In the privacy of my room, I broke down and sobbed.

Mark spent the whole night with me. I lay awake worrying about my babies, and about how the kids were getting along at home. When the light of dawn finally peeked through the window, I felt a little better emotionally. Daytime meant that Tommy would soon be off to school; Jeff, Kyle and Jessica would get some respite from the burden of taking care of him. Flowers and toys started arriving from friends and family. That served to cheer me up, but without my babies in my room, I felt distanced from the feeling of celebration.

My dad always told me, "You learn from adversity." He was absolutely right, but I never could quite figure out why it was being heaped on us. Kristen had developed spells of apnea, having to be stimulated by the nurses to make her start breathing again. She was averaging two spells a night. I was always paranoid over the possibility of crib death with all my babies, but now I was getting extremely panicky. Apnea scared me to death. Somehow, I just knew I wouldn't be doing any sleeping in the first year of Kristen's life. That was fine with me. I silently vowed that when she came home, I would watch her breathe all night long.

I had made the mistake of assuming that I was bringing the babies home when my four days in the hospital were over. It was not to be. The doctor informed me that they would be in the hospital for another two weeks. Nothing could have prepared me for the grief I felt at having to leave them behind.

The drive home was pretty quiet, except for the muffled whisper of my sobs. Jessica, Jeff and Kyle greeted me with big smiles and lots of tight hugs. They had cleaned the house from top to bottom, everything was sparkly clean, and being home again felt both wonderful and sad at the same time.

Mark had some errands to run. My own pillow felt soft against my face as I settled in to take what I thought would be a nap. Tommy's fits while I was at the hospital had been pretty much nonstop during his time awake. Realizing that his father had left the house, the roar of his rage rang through the entire dwelling. Jessica came running back to my room and got me. When I got to his bedroom door, he screamed at the top of his lungs, "I'm gonna kill your babies, you fucking bitch!"

My knees felt weak and I began to tremble. I hobbled back to my room and collapsed on the bed. Tears ran down my cheeks, already reddened from days of crying aloud over the babies' problems. Hearing me cry, Jessica came in and lay gently down beside me, her warm body against mine as she stroked my hair to comfort me. I felt so proud of my daughter. She had an inner strength that often reminded me of my mother. It was truly a gift.

My thoughts turned back to Tommy. Exhausted from trying to cope, I just couldn't see even the faintest flicker of hope where Tommy was concerned. I felt that I needed to concentrate my energies on the new babies. Instead, it was again focused only on Tommy and his perpetual violent rage.

There were times when I looked at Tommy and saw the face of a frightened little boy, but most times I saw evil in his face. Glimpses of the sweet innocent child inside were, unfortunately, rare. When he was peaceful I would often attempt to hold him and offer comfort, but invariably make things worse. It was strange: Our love for Tommy made him hate us that much more, while those with no emotional attachments to him were spared the brunt of his rage. Those who loved him were the focus of his hate. The harder we tried to love him, the more he punished us. It was paradoxical and there was nothing we could do to change it. Each night, I prayed that the next day Tommy would awaken and finally understand that we were only trying to help him, but each morning I found my prayers unanswered.

Mark and I spent the next two weeks going back and forth to the hospital to see our new babies. After a week, they finally let me breast-feed Megan. She was the healthier of the two babies and she took to the breast right away. Kristen followed two days later. Both had choking problems as they nursed, but the hospital staff was wonderful about trying to comfort me. They taught me what to do about the choking, and the hospital even gave us an infant CPR class. Megan was finally ready to go home a couple of days after her first breast feeding. Kristen a short while later.

Our doctor arranged for a portable apnea monitor so we could check on Kristen's breathing problems. Many nights it would pierce the quiet, startle us awake and into action. We'd jostle Krissie a little and she would be fine. She and Megan rarely slept anyway, so I never really entered deep sleep. When I did sleep, I was always listening for the monitor to go off. The constant wait for the next alarm was nerve wracking and even the sound of the phone ringing made my heart start pounding. The monitor was supposed to bring us peace of mind and on some level it did. We knew as long as she was on the monitor that we would know if she faced a crisis. Unfortunately, it also made us nervous wrecks with every shrill blast. Each alert in the middle of the night left us unable to return to sleep. I spent many nights just watching the flashing lights, waiting.

Meanwhile, things with Tommy were worse than they'd ever been. My heart pounded in my chest with fear whenever he was in the same room. Overwhelmed by caring for the twins, I wished so much that he would somehow realize my exhaustion and calm down. One morning getting Tommy ready for school, I turned around briefly to get his glasses off the fridge. Seizing the opportunity, he ran to Jake, grabbed him from behind and wrapped his arms tightly around Jake's waist from behind, his hands moving toward his genital area. Turning around, I leapt toward him, pulling Jake from his grasp. "Tommy, you know the rules. You are not to touch the other children." I sent him off to school. As the door closed behind him, my heart was racing. My hands were shaking as I called his father at work. Bursting into tears at the sound of Mark's voice, I stammered, telling him what had happened. "I am afraid of Tommy. I don't know how much more of this I can take." Sobs ripped through me as I spoke. I was scared to death of the present danger Tommy presented, as well as his potential for the future. I had read puberty usually made mental illness escalate. Tommy was growing rapidly and would soon be too big for me to be able to restrain him.

Soon after we brought the babies home, we received Tommy's new psychological evaluation. It indicated that the school thought we were being overly critical when we described his behavior. We had filled out a questionnaire, stating his behavior at home, for the school psychologist. As in the past, this psychologist had decided that she knew Tommy best based on his school behavior. But Tommy, we knew, had been on his honeymoon period during the evaluation; the psychologist hadn't seen any disturbing behaviors during her test. Based on her observations, her report stated that maybe we were "judging him too harshly based on his past behaviors." Reading her report, Mark and I both wished that she had to live with Tommy for a week. Her "expert" opinion would have done a complete flip-flop. She would have been less critical of us and more concerned with helping this very sick child.

By the time we had a conference to set up an individual education plan for Tommy, his teachers reported that he was having crying spells and being defiant every day in class. They completely dismissed the psychologist's report, labeling Tommy emotionally disturbed. We felt that because of the label, people would know to watch out for the other students around him or so we thought.

During the period that followed the conference, more trouble appeared. The week before Halloween was especially bad with Tommy spending the afternoons screaming in his room, and violently kicking his walls. On Saturday, he did this for the entire day. Then, as if to punctuate his fit of rage, he urinated all over the clean clothing that I had just put in his room. Then he put the stuff back on the shelf as if nothing had happened. It took several days to discover where the stench of urine was coming from. And when we questioned him he claimed no memory of the act.

On the day of Halloween, Tommy's behavior forced me to make a tough decision. Exhausted from his week-long barrage of cursing, death threats, urinating and violent tantrums, I made up my mind.

Tommy was not going trick-or-treating this year. Jeff volunteered to take him alone, but I refused. My mind was made up and backing down from my decision would have only shown weakness. That was something I didn't dare let Tommy see. I had to stick to what I had told Tommy. I knew it was the right decision. I had always made sure I was 100 percent consistent when it came to Tommy and I wasn't going to stop being that way now. Sure, I felt some guilt at depriving him of a childhood ritual, but his seriously bad behavior had to have consequences. Grounding a child from trick-or-treating was something I had never thought I would do, but with his terrible behavior, Tommy had backed me into a corner.

Halloween arrived and an air of tension filed the house. Kyle was a teenager and felt he was too old to go trick-or-treating. He dressed up like a monster to give out candy to the little children. He took great pains with his outfit, even draping cobwebs on his costume. Seeing my normally quiet son dressed in a monster costume, made me laugh.

Jake was dressed as Batman's sidekick Robin and Bobby was Spiderman. They looked like an adorable matched set of superheroes, as they were the same height. Bobby and Jake went trick-or-treating with Jeff, and Jessica left, in full Jester regalia, to join her friends, her first real sign that she was no longer a little girl.

However, the disappointment I felt over not being able to help Tommy celebrate the holiday made me feel miserable. Having such great kids reassured me that at least I had succeeded with the other seven. Unfortunately, that didn't make what I perceived to be my failure with Tommy any less painful.

The day after Halloween was my birthday. As I looked around the table at my children, my eyes fastened on Tommy. Often times I wondered what his reality was like. Was it scary? Was it a peaceful place inside of himself, all alone? Was he happy in his imaginary world? He never seemed nervous when confronted for doing anything wrong. It was as if someone else had done his misbehaviors and used his body without his permission. I knew deep down inside him that there was kindness buried, but I just couldn't bring it out to stay. Nothing we tried ever worked. That night, as I blew out the candles on my cake, I made my birthday wish. It wasn't the usual wish that we would all have many more years together. That year, I wished that we could find help for Tommy and that we would all be kept safe from him.

Thanksgiving was as chaotic as Halloween. Tommy urinated all over his room right before we served dinner, hosing down not only his entire bed, but also his clean clothing and toys. Christmas was coming in a month. His behavior always worsened between Halloween and New Year's and each of us dreaded the inevitable escalation in violence. Two days after Thanksgiving, we overheard him in his room saying that he hated Santa Claus.

During the next week Bobby reported to us that Tommy had begun hitting him at the bus stop. We tried to get him to stop. We even made him write over and over that he wouldn't hit Bobby, hoping against hope that it would sink in. His threats were becoming constant, with no end in sight. I called the insurance company for approval for Tommy to start seeing a psychiatrist. He badly needed to be on medication again, but money was a big problem for us. With formula and diapers piled onto our mountain of debt, scraping up twenty-five dollars a visit plus the co-payments for medication was going to be a struggle.

Unfortunately, after I described Tommy's problem none of the local providers on our insurance company's list would take him. They made excuses, such as "It's too far for you to drive to my office." I am certain the real reason was that they understood just how sick Tommy truly was and felt unable to adequately address the situation. There seemed to be no one to help Tommy, which increased the sense of isolation and hopelessness we already felt.

Finally, the insurance company talked a local non-contract psychiatrist into taking Tommy at their company's rate. His first appointment wasn't scheduled until his ninth birthday, January 26. That meant two months with no help, no medication, nothing. We were going to have to make it through Christmas. Our whole family, with the exception of Jake and the babies, who didn't understand, was filled with dread.

During the interim Tommy took his anger out on all of us, even his dad. He just didn't seem to care anymore. With his father now the main target of his attacks, we realized the rage inside Tommy was escalating to yet another new level. He screamed and cursed at Mark with a rage that had heretofore been reserved for the rest his family. Mark and I just didn't know what to do to stop him. Before our eyes, this child was sinking into a world of madness, a world that we were helpless to save him from. The impending psychiatric appointment was almost a month away, but at least we had an appointment. That gave us a small flicker of hope and we needed hope just to make it through.

Once again Christmas, was a trial. The mood wasn't festive. We kept our decorating traditions to a minimum to avoid setting Tommy off even more. Instead of putting the tree up at Thanksgiving as we usually did, we waited until the week before the holiday to decorate it, hoping to avoid at least some of Tommy's pre-Christmas anger pattern. The mood was very depressing. As if the emotional problems weren't taxing enough, we all ended up catching the flu. Ironically, Tommy never got sick. He was unbelievably physically healthy.

While Tommy opened his presents that Christmas morning, his face was totally expressionless as he methodically tore the wrapping from each one. Twitching and raging at the other children, he seemed to be having a psychotic episode. However, within the hour, he had put together perfectly all the Lego cars we had bought him. That was one of his strong points, being able to look at a picture and build something identical to it. He was good at that and I told him I was proud of him. He immediately began destroying what he'd created.

Throwing away the last of the torn wrapping paper, we took the presents to each child's room; we all felt relieved that the holiday was over. Once it had been my favorite time of year; now it was just too much stress. We took the tree down the day after Christmas. It was a beautiful tree, but I was glad to see it go. I didn't want anything to trigger Tommy's rage further. His illness was dragging the whole family down. By this point, we weren't sure anything ever could stop his pain or ours.

– chapter twelve –

Sad New Year

On January 20, 1999, Tommy left the bus stop and went to the neigh-borhood policeman's home, where he began constantly ringing their doorbell at 7:30 A.M. He was also throwing rocks at Bobby at the bus stop. A note from the bus driver informed me of all this, along with a patronizing comment that Tommy leaving the bus stop was a "safety hazard" and he had to notify me. I knew it was a safety hazard and it mortified me thinking of who Tommy might hurt next. The police offi-cer, who had a reputation for being extremely nice, apparently saw fit to forget the matter.

Four days later, Tommy's teacher sent home a note Tommy had written. It was about how much he hated a kid in his class named Pete. Two more days and he was scheduled to see a new psychiatrist. Just two more days! Frantically, I prayed to God to just let us get through those two more days!

Tommy saw his new psychiatrist on his ninth birthday. Dr. Tate was a young man who resembled Mark with his dark hair and full beard. He was a highly respected psychiatrist and well liked in the commu-nity. Mark took Tommy to his first appointment while I waited anxiously at home. It seemed to be hours before they returned.

Tommy stomped through the house, as usual, when he came in the door. Mark laid a bag of medication samples on the table. Our insurance wouldn't cover the anti-psychotic drug Zyprexia, which Dr. Tate had prescribed, and the doctor had given us these out of kindness. Dr. Tate had immediately realized the seriousness of Tommy's problems, which made Mark and me feel hopeful. He also gave us samples of another medication, Depakote, which was an anti-seizure medication that was also used to treat aggression. Finally, we had hope again. Zyprexia was a new medication, reputed to have already had relatively good success with schizophrenics. That boosted our hopes even further. Those moments when we had hope were so few and far between. For the first time in such a long time, we could breathe a little easier again.

Tommy's eyes seemed a little tired the next morning, but his psychotic look was still there. He threw rocks at the bus stop that morning. After school, I found his bookbag's side pocket crammed full of large rocks. Tommy told me, "I'm going to throw them all at Bobby and hit him." I shuddered as I took them away. Soon thereafter, the bus driver caught Tommy throwing rocks again and repeatedly kicking the neighbor's electrical box. This new medication didn't seem to help him at all.

Saturday he was furious that he was out of school for the weekend. His death threats peppered the air throughout the day. We overheard him having graphic conversations with the "Devil," about how he planned to kill us all. This behavior continued all weekend long. After a few days, the doctor added Depakote on top of the Zyprexia. I hoped that the new combination of medication would work their magic.

Tommy seemed a little shaky on the Depakote at first, but his aggressive behavior showed no signs of waning. He was still angry at Bobby, who, being extremely passive, was the perfect victim It made me physically sick to send Bobby out of the house with Tommy, but the school had given me no choice, since they would not provide Bobby with a separate bus. I prayed for the angels to watch over Bobby and I watched them till the two boys were out of sight.

That evening Tommy was supposed to do a poster of his family as a homework project, but I decided he shouldn't participate because of the repercussions I was afraid we would have if he did. Just knowing he was studying the family at school kept me on pins and needles.

Much to my dismay, his teacher let him do the poster at school. Tommy's poster was of five stick people lying on the ground, labeled Mark, Bobby, Jessica, Jeff and Beth. His interpretation caused me more worry.

On Valentines Day, he brought home a paper that he had written which simply stated, "Kimberly will not play with me on the playground." His teacher later told me that he had some kind of a crush on the girl. Kimberly must have realized Tommy was not normal. A part of me hurt for Tommy.

We saw Dr. Tate on the fifteenth of February for a medication check and the doctor decided to up Tommy's dosage of Depakote. After the appointment, Tommy stomped into the house as though he was invading a war zone and Mark followed close behind. Recognizing his aggressive walk, I quickly went to his book bag and searched for potential weapons. It was in his bag that I found the most disturbing picture I had ever seen.

Tommy had drawn an evil-looking and extremely detailed picture of the devil. The devil was standing over a grave deep underneath the green ground on which he stood. Inside the grave were two primitive stick figures holding swords. A house in the picture was in flames. When I questioned him about it, he told me that he wanted to set our house on fire. My fear turned to sheer terror that day. His eyes were as cold as ice.

That day I learned I had something new to fear: Tommy's desire to burn the house down. Realizing the risk, I began searching his clothing every day for matches. We'd always had to frisk him for weapons after school, but the idea that he might start a fire was far more frightening. One little match in the hands of a psychotic child could cause so much devastation. Frisking him made me feel sick inside, but I had to make sure he hadn't brought anything into the house that could hurt someone. Often times, he would make weapons out of parts of toys he had broken. Tommy seemed to be able to make weapons out of anything. We were not safe at all, nor was there any peace in our lives with Tommy at home.

My worry over Bobby's safety was ever on the rise. The school personnel always turned deaf ears when we tried to tell them that Tommy was dangerous. Tommy could bring on the tears when asked about doing something wrong and easily manipulate them into thinking that he was truly remorseful. We knew differently, however, and his phony tears didn't fool us.

In the coming days his rage against Bobby escalated. Tommy began hitting Bobby with his fists at the bus stop. Soon we heard that he actually sat on Bobby and pummeled him with his fists. Bobby didn't do anything to protect himself and Tommy took full advantage of his passivity. We disciplined Tommy every day by making him write, over and over, that he should not hit his brother at the bus stop. We grounded him for long periods of time. He didn't seem to care. Nothing worked.

Bobby began regressing. We had spent four years potty training him, but Tommy's attacks took all that away again. I felt sorry for Bobby and guilty that I couldn't be there to protect him. I was doing everything I felt I could possibly do, but I just couldn't stop Tommy.

Three days later, Bobby began telling us that Tommy was touching his penis at the bus stop, and when I asked Tommy about it, uncharacteristically, he turned on the tears and admitted doing it. I felt nausea well up inside me. He was not only molesting Bobby, but he was doing it in public. He didn't even fear getting caught. His impulses overrode his ability to care. We had kept Tommy from molesting Bobby after we first realized he was doing it, when he was four. Years of keeping him from molesting Bobby had not served to make the behavior go away, it had only denied him the opportunity to fulfill his impulses. Now he knew we couldn't protect Bobby from him when they were at the bus stop alone. Ever the opportunist, Tommy took full advantage of the situation. Tommy began doing it every morning they went to school. Tommy even boasted to me one day in March that he had touched Bobby's penis, telling me point blank that he would do it again. The explanation he gave for his behavior was, "Rod did it to me, so I do it to Bobby." In his damaged mind, that excuse seemed to justify what he was doing. The abused had become the abuser.

Early in March, I got a note telling me that Tommy had hit a car at the bus stop with a bottle he had thrown. The angry mother driving the car had confronted the bus driver with this information that morning. There was no question that he had done it deliberately. The school didn't punish him, they merely sat him down and told him not to do it again. He promised he wouldn't.

It seemed that each time he was allowed to get away with something, Tommy did something more risky. In a sense, the school not disciplining him was like giving him permission to keep on acting out in a violent way. The molestation of Bobby continued. We tried to discipline Tommy for his transgressions, but it was useless. Mainly for the safety of the other children, he was perpetually grounded. He was an ever-present danger when he was around them. I asked myself why Bobby and my other children should be put in a position where they were subjected to such emotional and physical terrorism just because they lived in the same house. We had gotten the impression from previous psychiatric hospitalizations that because he wasn't molesting "outsiders," we should always take him back home and see if he did it again. The children weren't guinea pigs to see if Tommy was a budding child molester. If a neighborhood boy were doing this to my kids, the police would have arrested him. Past history had led me to believe that no one would take the molestation of a family member as seriously as the molestation of someone outside the family.

Sending him to the hospital for a short time always seemed to leave him angrier when he returned home. The fear of making him more aggressive kept me from begging Dr. Tate to hospitalize him. Of course, we told him everything Tommy was doing. The doctor initiated the process of getting us state help through Medicaid and he also provided information for us to look into getting Tommy in the *Willie M.* program for violent children. This program would open the doors for state aid. Obtaining financial help was the only way we could afford to hospitalize him and that was obviously going to take time.

When Dr. Tate saw Tommy in mid-March, we told him about Tommy's continuing molestation of Bobby. Dr. Tate thought we should lessen the dosage of Depakote until Tommy was off of it. We reported Tommy still was urinating on his stacks of clean clothing in his room. Mark gave him the details of Tommy talking about a devil who "lives inside my forehead and tells me to do bad things." The pictures of the devil were beginning to appear on lots of his schoolwork. He drew two different devils and one had a long tail that looked like a penis hanging between his legs. Judging by his behavior, it wasn't so farfetched that maybe two devils actually did live inside of his head.

His progress report came in from his special forty-five minutes-a-day class to help him deal with frustration. That class and speech therapy were the only services the school was providing him. An unusual comment on the report made me wonder. "Tommy continues to work toward controlling his anger and is now taking time to 'cool off.' He expresses what makes him angry or how he feels." This had to mean that he was acting up in school if he had to take a "cooling off" period. Why weren't we hearing about this from the school? They never told us anything concrete regarding his behavior. I asked Tommy about the comment. His response was, "I push the other students around, even when I am not in a bad mood, sometimes." Forty-five minutes worth of class per day to help him with his intense and psychotic anger was pathetically inadequate. If talking to Tommy could have fixed his problems, I would have talked till I turned blue. I know they meant well, but it just wasn't helping. Would anything?

chapter thirteen

Madness and Mayhem

The cycles were deteriorating. Tommy was now telling us that a child named Temmy lived inside of him, as well as a caveman. He said they protected him from the devil. I noticed that a spelling paper he brought home had the name Temmy Henry on it. When I asked Tommy to tell me about Temmy, he began telling me about a seven-year-old child that lived in his head. He said that Temmy couldn't spell well. Judging by the spelling test with Temmy's name on it, he was right. I thanked him for telling me about Temmy and left the room wondering if this was merely the imagination of a psychotic child or if there were different personalities really living inside his tormented mind.

Tommy's conversations with the devil were becoming more frequent. He kept telling the devil that he loved him and wanted to play with him. He also seemed to be talking to someone else, who I assumed was either Temmy or the caveman Tommy told me about. Tommy said he could see these other entities do things. To Tommy, they were real people. He described the devil as red and very mean. The caveman had swords to protect him. Tommy said he could hear their voices telling him what to do. Shivers ran up my spine when he told me that the devil rubbed his back at night to make him go to sleep.

My suspicion was that Tommy had multiple personalities. He seemed to change so dramatically sometimes, in his speech, his walk, his facial expressions and sometimes even in his looks. The changes were dramatic, particularly his eyes. They seemed to change right before me, looking like the eyes of a different person, not the eyes of Tommy Henry. Sometimes he seemed like a small child, other times like a strong adult and often like evil incarnate. I had grown to know his personality changes from years of observation. Tommy's different personalities could be easily recognized by the different ways that he would look, walk and talk. I could readily pinpoint a "danger day" just by looking at his eyes. When one eye was aiming inward and the other looking straight ahead, it was time to watch out: An explosion of rage was imminent. Dr. Benson used to tell me that he seemed to have a personality that got him through the school day. That hadn't changed over the years. Tommy always seemed to be able to keep himself together and control his inner demons better at school than he did at home. It was as if I sent an innocent, baby-like child out the door every morning, and an evil entity got off the bus every afternoon. When he got home, the baby would be gone. Someone else would come bursting through, venting his terrible rage. This whole thing was so weird that I felt like an idiot telling people my theory. I pretty much kept it to myself for fear of not being believed.

Two days after my conversation with Tommy regarding Temmy, I gave him a pencil and paper and I asked him to write down the names and ages of all the people that lived inside him. My eyes widened with amazement as I watched him write down five names and ages, including a child named Thomas. During his last psychiatric appointment, he had told the doctor that he had a friend named Thomas who lived in his bedroom with him. The doctor had asked him if Thomas was a pretend child or a real child. Tommy had told him he was real.

Tommy had written that Temmy was seven, Thomas was eight, the devil was twenty-seven, the caveman was twenty-eight and Tommy (himself) was nine. I stood there staring at the paper. Tommy turned around, his voice startling me out of thought. He looked up at me matter-of-factly, pointed to the word "caveman" on his paper, telling me that the caveman was a little older than the devil. In that moment

Tommy's voice and mannerisms sounded like an adult. His observation was correct. The caveman was a year older than the devil on the paper. Practically speechless from what I had just seen, I thanked Tommy, quickly leaving his room with the paper and pencil. Outside his door, I braced myself against the wall, my heart pounding inside my chest. At that moment, I knew that to Tommy this was all very real. I took the paper and showed it to Mark. It disturbed him as much as it did me. We both knew Tommy was sinking into a mad world. We were scared for him, as much as we feared for ourselves. How do you save a child who is sinking into the depths of madness?

Meanwhile, Tommy was getting more violent at the bus stop. He continued to beat up and molest Bobby. That afternoon he used the bathroom and, an hour later, threw his clean clothing all over the floor and peed all over it. He had a bad day at school, according to his pink behavior sheet. There was an "R" for respect on it. That meant that he had disrespected someone. We found a pencil hidden in his book bag. Was Bobby his intended stabbing target? His "take home" folder had some new artwork on it. Tommy had drawn the devil, with long claws, on the front of his folder.

The next day was just as bad. Tommy was touching Bobby's penis again. Without reason, he threw Bobby down at the bus stop, taking his glasses and deliberately bending the frames. There was another "R" on his pink sheet when he came home that afternoon. Someone at school had again been treated disrespectfully. Tommy claimed that the "R" was for pushing some of his friends around. He claimed he did it because he was in a bad mood. Upset, I sent him straight to his room. There, he deliberately urinated on his clean clothing, just as he had the day before. That afternoon, we overheard him saying, "I love you, devil."

The morning after that, Tommy was so angry he bent his own glasses until they broke. It felt as if I was being ripped apart inside every time I had to send the boys to the bus stop. We couldn't be there to protect Bobby or to stop Tommy from attacking his little brother: Mark had to work, and I was stuck inside with the twins. Day after day it was more of the same.

Soon Bobby told us that Tommy was inappropriately touching a kindergartner at the bus stop. After that shocking revelation, the pendulum of impending disaster that I always felt hanging over our heads was now swinging deathly close. The simple ringing of the phone or the doorbell made me jump, sending my heart racing wildly. Each day, I expected a call or a visit from some irate parent, their child the victim of my disturbed stepson. Who could blame them? Their children were going to school with a child who molested other children. The fear of lawsuits constantly crossed my mind, rattling me further. With eight kids, we didn't have any money. There was no way we could afford a lawyer if we got sued because of Tommy. Fearing that he was molesting others was making me feel unbearably desperate. We had to get Tommy to a permanent safe place where he could be treated.

Overwhelmed with fear, Mark and I called Tommy's therapist at the local mental health center and Mark went there so that he could apply for the *Willie M.* certification. We needed the state's help desperately. The program would put Tommy under the care of a case manager, with Medicaid and the state paying for everything he needed to treat his violent behaviors. This included medical testing, psychiatric care, medications, hospitalization and even group homes and therapeutic foster care, until the age of eighteen. We knew it was our only hope. Our insurance had a $16,000 lifetime cap on mental health. That would only cover about fifteen days in the mental hospital. That would be just enough time to set Tommy off and when they sent him back home, he would be angrier and more violent than ever.

The therapist must have sensed the desperation in my voice. She talked with me for almost an hour. Tears turned to racking sobs, as I told her what we were going through and how afraid we all were. Gently, she suggested that we might want to think about temporarily hospitalizing Tommy. "It does no good," I told her tearfully, "he has never been kept in the hospital long enough to help him before. Tommy always ends up angrier when he comes home than when he goes in and that increases the danger to our family." Even though temporary hospitalization would give us a short break, the aftermath of his return home seemed too high a price to pay for a limited time without him. We felt the *Willie M* program was our only hope.

When I got off the phone I began punching my pillow. Years of pent-up frustration poured from my clenched fists as they pummeled angrily away at my inanimate target. I couldn't fix this child! Dear God in Heaven, I couldn't fix Tommy! I wasn't even sure I could keep trying any longer. My resolve was leaving me, draining away more with every day that passed. Overwhelmed by the intensity of my pain, I called my "therapist," my mom, and poured out my heart to her, as I often did during these trying times. Always knowing just what to say, she told me, "Stay focused, Beth, just stay focused." I tried rooting her words firmly in my mind. "Focus, Beth, just stay focused," I said to myself, over and over.

The next day, things just got worse. Tommy brought home a picture of a house that looked like it was being consumed by fire. He also brought home a picture of a devil attached to a story about how much he hated our cat. We hadn't allowed Tommy near the animals for several years. Judging by his picture, he was obviously fixating on them again. He seemed fascinated at that point with killing things: himself, animals and his family. My mind flashed back to all the times he tried to choke our cats and puppies. I also had found out from his younger brother that Tommy had sat on him as he lay helplessly on the ground that morning. He pummeled him in the face with his fists. Bobby's extremely small stature made him virtually defenseless against Tommy, who was twice his size. After beating his brother, he had stuck his hand in Bobby's pants and played with his penis. Now when I began questioning him about this, he stuck his hands into his own pants and began furiously masturbating in front of me. When I asked him about what had happened at the bus stop, and how he'd acted with Bobby that day, Tommy became enraged and head-butted my face. His attack was so sudden that it left me defenseless. There was a bruise and a swollen knot forming on my jaw.

One of the children's mothers had caught Tommy at the bus stop exposing himself to other children. I asked myself why she didn't call the school and report him. Getting into real trouble may have helped bring the seriousness of this situation to light, as far as the school was concerned. There was no doubt in my mind that he would target children again!

This wasn't the first time I had to recover from his assaults. The pain in my jaw brought back painful memories. Three years before, in Virginia, he had put my wrist in a cast for eight weeks during one of his violent fits. As soon as the cast came off, he re-injured it again. Now, I had no choice but to walk away and call my mother to vent.

Still nursing my wound with a bag of ice, I cried when my husband came home from work, and told him that he hadn't been there to protect me. That just heaped more onto Mark's already overflowing plate of guilt. In truth, I didn't blame Mark. He had to work to feed our family. My precious husband was just doing the best he could. I wanted so much to make that hurt in his eyes go away, but I couldn't. He couldn't fix Tommy any more than I could. We both hurt so deeply and just didn't know what to do to help this child.

However, I was beginning to face the fact that it was all up to me, the painful decision would be mine. I was going to have to do something to see that we would be safe in our own home.

Tommy now claimed that the devil was the one touching others. Each time he told me this, I would pick up his hands, put them up to his face and tell him he was responsible for whatever he did with these hands. Tommy laughed.

During the next few days, the bus driver decided to put Tommy and Bobby together on the bus. When I found out about this, I was livid. The driver effectively made Bobby easy prey by giving Tommy unsupervised access to him. Mark called the school, emphatically telling them again he wanted the boys separated on the bus. At least when Bobby went to school, he would be sitting somewhere else.

Monday came and we took Tommy to see Dr. Tate. He wanted to add a new medication, Buspar, in a week, as well as first upping the Depakote again for aggression. We told Dr. Tate about the devil, Temmy and the caveman, as well as about how Tommy spoke of the devil being the one who was touching Bobby. Mark also mentioned that Bobby was telling us that Tommy was molesting another child at the bus stop."Tommy also told us that he heard the devil telling him what to do." The doctor took it all in, seeming concerned, but not panicked. Again, Mark and I left the office with instructions to increase Tommy's medication. Dr. Tate had mentioned that maybe we needed to start thinking again about hospitalization for Tommy. The doctor, realizing our financial predicament, had been waiting on our ability to get state help. While I was grateful that he understood our problems, I felt frustrated that Dr. Tate hadn't told us to put Tommy in the hospital immediately.

On the other hand, we wondered if maybe not hospitalizing Tommy somehow indicated that his problems weren't as bad as we thought they were. Sexually molesting his brother, and possibly another child, seemed serious to me. Hearing stories like ours over and over could certainly desensitize a person. Maybe it was that he just didn't want to make us feel worse than we already did. Maybe he just thought that medication would eventually get all of this under control. Whatever he was thinking, we were the ones living the nightmare. The opinions of others, professionals or otherwise, didn't make our heartache and fear any less. Mark and I felt utterly alone.

We had another issue with which to contend. Tommy had recently been trying to lure Bobby into his room. The cry, "Come here, Bobby, I want to kill you!" would often chillingly reverberate through our house. We tried to keep a more vigilant watch on Bobby than ever. He was trusting enough to make himself vulnerable to Tommy's sinister requests. Bobby had been showing increased signs of post-traumatic stress disorder, crying all the time and acting like an infant. The skin was gone from his fingers where he had chewed it off, causing his fingers to swell and ache. He was biting his tiny forearms until he left tooth-mark bruises all over them. Tommy was taking Bobby down with him and we were trying to hold onto the poor child for dear life.

Tommy told us that he hated Bobby because he was so mean. Bobby had to be the most docile child on the face of the Earth, but not in Tommy's warped fantasies. One morning, feeling premonitions of terrible events to come, I sent Bobby to the bus stop with Tommy. My hands were noticeably shaking. There was a quivering feeling inside the pit of my stomach. He looked so small and vulnerable. I prayed to the good Lord to watch over him and protect him from his brother. Tears welled up in my eyes as he vanished from my sight with Tommy. Something was going to happen again, I could just feel it. Inside me was an overwhelming feeling of anxiety that never abated.

A sick feeling came over me as I watched the kitchen clock tick by the hours. As the two hands reached the designated time that the boys would be home, I was feeling totally rattled and queasy. Once again Bobby came in the door telling me that Tommy had molested him and a kindergarten child, as well. Careful not to ask leading questions, I simply asked Tommy to tell me what had happened at the bus stop and on the bus. He looked straight at me and unemotionally said, "The devil played with Bobby's penis and (another child's) penis too." He also said the devil played with the penis of another little boy and the "privates" of a little girl who sat with him on the bus. Bobby had been prevented from sitting beside Tommy on the bus after our call to the school. We had wrongly assumed they would have Tommy sit by himself, based on the inappropriate touching concerns we had told them about. Instead, Tommy was sitting beside innocent young victims.

Wanting to find out what was really going on, I put Jeff on a stake-out in his parked car, fifty feet from the bus stop. Tommy had no idea that he was being watched.

It wasn't long till Jeff saw him begin running after the little kinder-garten boy, seemingly in innocuous play, grabbing him from behind, wrapping his hands tightly around the child's waist. Tommy got the child to stand still. My stepson came around to the front of the child and kneeled before him, placing his hands on the boy's crotch. Seeing what was happening, Jeff leapt out of the car and raced to the bus stop. Tommy was startled to see that he had been caught. Jeff admonished Tommy, ordering him to keep his hands to himself.

Jeff went back to his car and continued watching Tommy. He had warned Tommy that he would be watching him until the bus arrived. A short while later, Tommy tried to lure the same little boy behind some bushes, out of Jeff's sight. Again, Jeff bolted from his car and ran to the bus stop, this time instructing Tommy to wrap his hands around and hold on to the metal stop sign post until the bus came. Angry at Tommy's open defiance of his previous order, Jeff told Tommy he would be watching him every day from now on. His plans aborted because of his older brother, Tommy gave Jeff an evil gaze. There was an explosive anger boiling inside him; he had been caught, his impulse to molest unfulfilled.

I hated to burden Jeff with watching Tommy, but I had no other choice. I had to take care of the younger children. I was greatly relieved that he was there at the bus stop watching. My hopes of reassurance turned to grief, however, when Jeff came home and informed me that he had witnessed Tommy inappropriately touching other children. I had to do something about it, right now! Stepmother or not, I was mak-ing the decision to put Tommy in the hospital, right now! We couldn't let this happen anymore. This had to stop, for the sake of Tommy, the other children and my entire family. I called Tommy's therapist. She told me we needed to hospitalize him immediately.

She also instructed me to call the school right away and emphatically tell them about Tommy's inappropriate behavior. The therapist told us to insist that he needed a seat alone on the bus that afternoon. He also needed to go the bathroom alone, with no other children present. As per her instructions, I told them that he had to be watched at all times. Taking action made me feel so much better than helplessly floundering in a sea of "What do I do?"

Making sure that Tommy was in a program that treated kids who sexually molested others now became a primary concern. Someone had previously given me the name of a program for youthful sex offenders in eastern North Carolina. I called the director. Unfortunately, his program was for children twelve and up. Tommy was only nine. After listening intently to my story, the man told me that I should look into the program for sexually reactive children at a mental hospital in western North Carolina. The doctor there was a chemical expert when it came to kids like Tommy. He said that this hospital was excellent. I felt this was my chance to get Tommy the specific kind of help he so desperately needed.

Not waiting for Mark's permission, knowing he would support my decision fully, I decided to call. Several calls later, the hospital began working on getting insurance approval for admission. They said they would call me that evening.

When Tommy came home that afternoon, he looked directly into my eyes. My stepson began telling me that the devil had touched the penis of the little boy he sat with on the bus that day. The school hadn't listened to me. Tommy was still sitting with other children on the bus. Why? Didn't they see I was trying to protect the other children? As if extremely proud of what he had done, he bragged that Jeff had caught him trying to touch the kindergartner penis.

The hospital didn't call. I cried all night long, wondering if I was doing the right thing. When I told Mark, he was supportive, but I still felt very alone. Was I making the right decision? Would this hospital be different? Would they actually help my stepson or would he just return home in a few weeks, angry and out for blood? My mind replayed these thoughts like a broken record till dawn.

Then around noon the phone rang. It was the hospital. We finally had the go ahead to admit Tommy, but even though we had gotten him qualified for Medicaid since he needed hospitalization for at least a year, it would only be for two weeks unless the *Willie M.* program admitted him. *Willie M.* certification was named after a class action lawsuit against the state. The state agreed to provide appropriate services to violent children, regardless of their ability to pay, as a settlement to the lawsuit. The program could help children like Tommy and their families. Getting in the program took several weeks, lots of information and intricate forms. A review committee would decide if Tommy was eligible, after carefully scrutinizing medical and school records and his very detailed application. Hospitalizing Tommy would provide more documentation of his condition for the committee. That, in turn, would help Tommy.

Mark picked Tommy up from school and brought him home. I had already packed his clothing, making sure his name was on each item. Tommy seemed accepting of the fact that he was being hospitalized again. Mark ate lunch and packed the car in a silence that spoke volumes. Tommy waited in his room. I found myself pacing the kitchen floor, once again wondering if this was the right thing to do. Self-doubt was gnawing at me. A part of me felt like I had failed Tommy.

A penetrating sense of sadness hung over me that day; a sadness that would take weeks to go away. When Mark left him at the hospital, Tommy simply said "Bye, Dad." That was all. Mark said there was no emotion in Tommy's voice.

In the quiet of the next morning, my body felt lighter than air when I walked. I noticed simple things that I hadn't noticed in so long. I saw the sunshine beaming in through the windows. The rays felt warm and invigorating. Cute things about the babies that I hadn't had time to look at before, thrilled me. Finally being able to spend time just playing with them without the persistent interruption of Tommy's fits was an amazing blessing that I suddenly cherished. Tommy had taken so much of our time and energy that the simple pleasures in life had been completely forgotten. Experiencing those pleasures again with a heightened sense of feeling was remarkable.

I found myself watching the clock all weekend, just thinking about what I should be doing for Tommy at that moment. Our whole lives had revolved around his rigid routine. The extra time I found in the day was strangely disconcerting, yet joyful. While we all tried to enjoy the peace in our home, a cloud of fear still waited in the wings. If Tommy wasn't admitted to the *Willie M.* program, he would be home in about two weeks, as he had with past hospitalizations. That was terrifying in light of our newfound freedom. Having freedom is bittersweet when you know you will only lose it again.

On Monday, I called Tommy's teacher, Jane Greer, to let her know that he was in the hospital. We had an eye-opening conversation. I told her what Tommy had been doing to Bobby on the bus and at the bus stop, as well as giving her a brief overview of what he had been doing at home, to the family. When I told her about Tommy exposing himself, she said, "I knew he was doing that last fall, but not recently." I struggled to continue the conversation. Why hadn't someone let me know this last fall?

Ms. Greer told me that she had been "walking on eggshells" with Tommy that whole year. He had been having crying fits whenever he didn't get his way or was just plain angry. Tommy had been accusing the other children of doing things that hadn't happened. One little girl had even been called to the guidance office because of Tommy's wild accusations. They knew Tommy was lying and that the little girl had done nothing, but they simply talked to Tommy without disciplining him at all.

Showing obvious signs of emotional disturbance, he told the other children that he hated them, often suddenly yelling this out in the middle of class. His teacher told me that the other students had been forgiving of Tommy, but that recently even their patience had worn thin. His teacher felt that third grade would be very difficult for Tommy because of his behavior problems. I whole-heartedly agreed. The school couldn't keep him back in second grade another year, because they "socially promoted" kids. He had to be kept with other students around his own age. Tommy's grades were below average; he was functioning on a kindergarten level, but social promotions prevented him from being held back. This was frustrating, to say the least.

Ms. Greer also told me about a disturbing incident. Of course, no detailed notes ever came home to really tell me what he was doing in class. We had no idea that his whole class had pretty much been at his mercy. One day, Tommy had been about to hit a child in the lunch line. Seeing his balled-up fist clenched and poised to strike, his teacher stepped between the two boys to protect the other child from getting hit. In his frustration at being thwarted, Tommy turned to the cafeteria wall. There he began beating his head against it, loudly proclaiming he was stupid and bad. Why in the world hadn't anyone told me this was going on? We had assumed he was being relatively good in school when, in fact, he was disturbing his class and displaying out-of-control behavior on a regular basis.

The next day the school guidance counselor called, emphatically telling me "the school hadn't seen any bad behaviors." When I told her about what Tommy's teacher had told me during our extensive conversation the day before, she turned cold. She quickly back pedaled, admitting that there had been one incident recently, in which Tommy accused a little girl of doing something that she hadn't. Both kids had been called to the office and Tommy had been "talked to."

The guidance counselor's feeble attempts to deny Tommy's disturbed behaviors really made me feel both hurt and angry. I pointed out to her that the safety of the other children was paramount. She agreed, saying that would be an important issue in determining placement for Tommy next year. She requested a consent form to talk to Tommy's doctors. Mark signed the papers that evening. We needed the school to be honest about Tommy on the *Willie M.* paperwork, but I sensed they were afraid of lawsuits. The bus stop, as well as the bus itself, was considered to be "school grounds." The school system could be held liable for any incidents of violence or abuse. Judging by my conversation with the counselor, they seemed to have clammed up tightly in the anticipation of a potential lawsuit. I asked myself why they couldn't see that helping Tommy so that other children were protected was the most important thing.

As the next week passed, I felt better seeing Bobby go to and from the bus stop in safety. My own nausea and shakiness subsided. I truly cherished those special moments, seeing Bobby come in the door smiling every afternoon. Knowing he was safe meant so much to me.

We talked to Tommy on the phone several times since hospitalizing him. He never asked about the family. We hadn't heard from his doctor in over a week. I was getting nervous that they would only see his usual "honeymoon period" and send him home.

Tommy's therapist at the hospital, Ronnie, called and asked me some questions. Having been up all night with the babies, sleep deprivation clouded my mind. I didn't feel that I expressed everything I wanted her to know. When I told her about Tommy's "devil," she said, "I'll just write 'patient is obsessed with the devil' in his chart." That left me wanting to cry. That wasn't what I meant at all. I had been trying to explain his hallucinations, not simply a fixation. Self-doubt was already running a marathon through my head as I hung up the phone. Did these people really have a clue as to what they were actually dealing with? Ronnie asked me what Tommy's goals should be in the hospital. Bluntly, I told her, "they would be that he should stop molesting people, as well as stop wanting to kill others." She seemed taken aback by my comment, but I was just telling the truth.

Tommy's *Willie M.* coordinator, Barbara, came out to the house to help me work on the package for the review committee. She was a warm, caring older woman who had a great deal of compassion for the families of the mentally ill. It was as if she knew exactly what we were going through. That made it so much easier to talk to her about Tommy. Barbara suggested I go back and write everything down that we had been through in the last year. That wasn't as hard as it sounded; everything seemed permanently etched into my brain. Barbara said this would help the committee understand what it felt like to be us, what it was like to live with Tommy and the environment of pain and fear that he created in our home. It drained me mentally to write it all down, but at the same time it felt like a much-needed emotional catharsis. It hurt to write about the past, but strangely, it felt liberating, too. Finally, I had my chance to make someone else understand my pain and the pain of my loved ones.

Mark paid a visit to the hospital. Tommy was beginning to get into fights with the adult male aides on the ward. While I was relieved that they were seeing his violent side, it really scared me that he had graduated to attacking total strangers, many of them huge, muscular young men. Still, I told myself they were seeing the real Tommy. That was exactly what they needed to see, in order to be able to help him appropriately.

Apparently, Tommy was upset over Temmy. Over lunch with his

father, he told Mark that he had "thrown Temmy out into the yard" the first day he came to the hospital. He said that when he did that, Temmy became a tree on the immaculately manicured grounds outside the hospital. Temmy, the tree, "talked" to Tommy when he went out to play. Then one morning a groundskeeper cut down the tree that Tommy thought was Temmy. To the groundskeeper, it was merely an eyesore to be eradicated; to Tommy, it was a real entity.

The nurse Mark spoke with about the incident said that Tommy had an "altercation." Hospitals always use fancy words to describe fights and other bad behaviors. Perhaps to the staff it makes it seem like the kids aren't as bad off when they use flowery language to describe violent outbursts, or maybe they are just trying to be kind to the parents, momentarily trying to downplay the seriousness of the child's illness. Who knows? They may use eloquent words, but they still mean the same thing: the child is violent and dangerous.

Mark spoke with Dr. Frank that afternoon. The doctor was quite surprised to hear about the conversation Mark had with Tommy, regarding Temmy. Tommy had told Dr. Frank that he wasn't hearing voices anymore. Hoping the medication he had placed Tommy on had already been effective, Dr. Frank was surprised to hear what Tommy had told Mark. I suspect that Dr. Frank learned a thing or two that day about how well Tommy could manipulate others. The disturbed little boy was protecting the only reality he had ever known.

Tommy started saying that Temmy, a child named Tyler, the caveman and the devil were dead. Not gone, but dead! It sounded like he had become fixated on death after the tree incident, even when it came to his own entities. When Barbara called that week, I could tell she was deeply concerned. The *Willie M.* paperwork hadn't come in from either the hospital or the school. The longer it took to get the information, the longer it would take to get *Willie M.* certification.

Our insurance company had rolled over to a new HMO policy that would now provide thirty-five days in the hospital for mental health inpatient treatment. This was an improvement, but I knew thirty-five days would run out quickly. Medicaid would have to take over. How long would they cover Tommy as an acute case? If he qualified for residential treatment, Medicaid would stop payment. The hospital would then have no choice but to send him home. What were we going to do?

I couldn't let that happen, I just couldn't! The anxiety over whether our coverage would run out was a constant worry. It weighed my shoulders down during the day, and kept me awake all night. After experiencing life without Tommy, how could we ever go back to the stress and constant fear of having him at home? How could I possibly let my children live in perpetual danger again? I knew I had to find a way. I couldn't give up now. Mom kept telling me to stay focused. I was trying with all my might to do just that. Failure was not an option.

On the fourteenth of the month, I saw our regular family practitioner. Sympathetically, he told me he had just read over Tommy's records, because Dr. Frank had called needing information from him regarding Tommy's history. Dr. Lyle said that he hadn't realized how bad things had been for us. Though graphic and terrifyingly explicit, the records didn't even begin to accurately reflect everything we had been through. Probably the world's best family practitioner, Dr. Lyle promised he would do everything he could to help keep our family safe. I valued his reassurance.

Tommy was babbling when Mark called him that evening. He asked his dad when he was coming to visit. Mark told him he would be there later that week. Tommy paused for a moment, then asked his dad when he was coming up to visit. Mark said sadly, "It was like he never even asked the first time. He seemed so out of it, like he wasn't really there."

Mark met with Dr. Frank the next afternoon. Mark noticed that Dr. Frank was looking exhausted. The burden of caring for sixty mentally ill children as the only psychiatrist on staff must have weighed heavily on the prematurely aging man. This compassionate doctor was determined to find the answers for the children in his care. It was apparent from his tired-looking appearance that he never rested until he found a way to help his young patients.

He said Tommy had been exhibiting paranoia. Tommy was accusing others, particularly the staff, of doing things that they had not done. Tommy had also been assaulting others, frequently having to be isolated to the quiet room. They were going to increase his dosage of Zyprexia, but I didn't feel like it was working for him at all. They had tried Respiradal the week before and he had a reaction to it. After Zyprexia, there would be Seroquel and, as a last resort, Clozaril.

I had read that Clozaril was a dangerous drug, but it had great success in schizophrenia cases where nothing else seemed to work. At least it offered some hope. The hospital told Mark, "As long as there was a payment source, Tommy can remain in the hospital." The bottom line was that it all came down to money and we didn't have any. We were scared and felt pressure to get *Willie M.* funding. That was the only hope we had, effectively increasing our feelings of desperation.

When Mark called Tommy again, Tommy told him he had a fight that morning, but now had "turned himself around." His new attitude didn't last till even the next morning. While playing football outside that morning, Tommy was accidentally hit in the face with the ball. Blinded by rage, Tommy fiercely pummeled the kid who threw the ball. Tommy's paranoia was readily apparent, as he swore that the kid had done it on purpose. When isolated in his room, he threw vehement tantrums for the rest of the day. His inner turbulence had been unleashed by a simple accident.

Mark asked him that night on the phone how Temmy and the caveman were. He said "Fine." When Mark told him that he had previously said they were all dead, he backtracked and said, "Yeah, yeah, they are dead. They are where God lives." Apparently he was trying to protect the voices by lying to Dr. Frank that he no longer heard them. It occurred to us that the "devil" was capable of being so manipulative that he would tell lies to keep the doctors from finding out about Tommy's other personalities.

A few days later, Medicaid papers arrived via mail informing us that they were now re-certifying Tommy's condition every two days, instead of just once a week. His time on Medicaid was running out. Feeling panicked, I called Barbara and told her what I felt was going on with Medicaid. She had even more upsetting news.

Finally, the school had returned the *Willie M.* paperwork. The part his regular teacher was to fill out was missing. His forty-five-minutes-a-day special-ed teacher had said she had seen no inappropriate behaviors, even after the "controlling his anger" comment on his progress report. The regular teacher's assistant had made one comment about Tommy kicking a child in the ribs and beating his own head on the wall. There was nothing about his paranoia, the crying fits in class or trying to hit other children. This gave both Barbara and me a sinking feeling. We had been counting on the school. Everything his teacher told me had been left out. I felt the reason was fear of being sued, but without the school contributing their knowledge of Tommy's behavioral and emotional problems, there would be more problems in getting him into the program. Even if there weren't, and we sent in his *Willie M.* paperwork now, it could take another month for approval. We were running out of time.

Mustering up all the bravery that I could, I placed a call to the director of Social Services in Raleigh. She wasn't in that day, but I spoke with her assistant, Claire. She seemed extremely sympathetic when I told her what we were going through. She was very concerned about protecting the other children in our home, and said she would make a few phone calls to see what she could do to help me. Her promise, to do what she could to help, made me feel a little better.

Barbara soon called and told me we had ten days to get a payment source. Tommy had met Criterion Five, which meant he now needed residential care. However, a time limit had been imposed. My own desperation had reached a low point. How could the sickest of the sick be turned away from the mental hospital because they were so mentally ill that they needed long-term care? The system made absolutely no sense whatsoever. I called Claire again. She made calls to our local mental health center and spoke with the director. Claire assured me that she fully understood the gravity of the situation. While her help meant volumes to me, my main problem still loomed large. How were we going to find a payment source in ten days?

Feeling overwhelmed, I called Barbara again. Barbara had been on the phone all morning trying to find a way to help us. Her inner strength and determination were inspirational to me, giving me a boost in my own courage to keep trying to find help. She suggested the state hospital as a possible transfer option. Medicaid would approve longer stays there because their rates were cheaper.

I resolved once again that, no matter what, I wasn't going to give up fighting to get Tommy the help he needed and to protect the lives of my other children.

Making phone call after phone call, I tried to get help. I called the local mental health offices, Barbara, Dr. Tate, the Governor's Advocacy Council and even the DSS. Then, in the blessed quiet of the middle of the night, an idea came to me that would change everything. I would write to my state senator and ask for help. There was certainly nothing to lose by trying. The next morning, on the Internet, I looked up addresses for my county's state legislators. There were pictures of both men on the computer screen. One of the two men had a kind face. On further investigation, I saw that he was an attorney and, as if by some miracle, on the State Health Committee; instinct told me that I had found the right man. I prayed that he would listen to a desperate mother's impassioned plea for her stepson and the safety of her family.

Before I knew it, my heart had been poured out into a three-page letter. I must have read it a hundred times, over and over, trying to reassure myself that I was doing the right thing. All I had to go on was raw emotion. Mark reviewed the letter, as did the older children, and based on their good comments, I sent the letter out the next morning. I felt a jolt when I heard the mail truck pull up to our mailbox and take the letter. There was no turning back now. "Please God, help me," I prayed, "please, protect my children. Please find a way to keep Tommy in the hospital till he gets help."

The next morning, I got a call from Barbara. She had called Tommy's teacher. The teacher had told her she hadn't seen a lot of bad behaviors, only a lot of crying. What happened to everything she told me? Frustration was welling up inside me. There was no way I had misunderstood anything Tommy's teacher had told me. She had given me specific details, which I had written down during our conversation. Taking notes during conversations helped me to accurately remember everything. The habit was well ingrained. Reviewing those notes only aggravated me further.

Barbara suggested that I place a call to the "troubleshooter" at the DSS office in Raleigh. Luckily, I got through to him on my first try. It just so happened that he had gotten the Criterion Five paperwork that morning. To my surprise, he explained that this was actually a "safety net." The kind man on the phone reassured me that he was fully aware that Tommy was a danger to the family. I exhaled a deep sigh as I hung up the phone. He was going to make a few calls. Someone would get back to me.

Barbara called later that day with encouraging news. She informed me that the director of the local mental health center had gotten us a case manager to make sure that a plan was in place if Tommy was to be discharged from the hospital. This was great news. It was a step in the right direction. It was help. Barbara gave me the case manager's number and I called her immediately. Voice mail greeted me on the line, I left my message, I hung up the phone and cried. An hour must have passed before the torrent of tears finally ceased. Strength renewed, I began thinking about my next course of action.

Laura, the case manager, called me the next morning. She was already looking into a transfer to the state hospital, as well as to a group home, should Tommy be prematurely discharged from the hospital. Her pulled together attitude and apparent compassion for my family gave me a sense of immediate trust in her. Someone else would now shoulder a portion of the burden. Knowing this, I could finally relax a little. There would still be calls to make, but not nearly as many. There was a plan quickly falling into place which was very reassuring.

Dr. Frank called me later that morning. He needed to start Tommy on Seroquel; the Zyprexia was doing nothing for him. Tommy was still having major screaming fits and not "limiting his boundaries." Dr. Frank said he hadn't molested anyone at the hospital; that was, of course, because he had the supervision of an entire staff all day. Given the opportunity, I felt he would have offended in a heartbeat. Medicaid had been contacted to ask for an extended stay. The hospital had tried our insurance company, but due to a "failure to pre-certify," Tommy had been denied three days of his 35-day limit. Dr. Frank told me that Tommy was very dangerous. He didn't want to send him home, because he knew he would molest Bobby or others again. Finally, the hospital had realized what I knew all along.

When I told the doctor about my problems with the school, he told me to let the school know that Tommy was very dangerous, that the other kids needed to be protected from him. I told him I felt like they were afraid we would sue them over what happened to Bobby. He said that I should tell them that while we wouldn't sue them, if Tommy doesn't get help and comes back to the school, other parents might sue the school for not protecting their kids from him. He sounded almost angry. Dr. Frank told me to tell them that the hospital would back me up. Wow, real passion coming from a psychiatrist. I had always thought they never got emotional about anything, but I realized I was wrong. It felt refreshing to see a doctor that cared so much.

Tommy had been diagnosed with a psychotic disorder, but the doctor was still unsure if it was schizophrenia or bi-polar disorder. Either way, he was psychotic and dangerous. Hanging up the phone, I finally felt like things were getting on the right track. They were seeing the real Tommy. The road ahead was still long and treacherous, but I wouldn't give up, not now.

When Mark called Tommy that night, the boy became incredibly belligerent. I was used to Tommy treating me this way, but he was almost always civil to his father. He was getting off topic throughout the conversation and could not be redirected. He said he had been to the time out room that day, but had turned his behavior around after lunch. Tommy had said the same thing several days earlier. Tommy would turn his behavior around, then do a complete 180-degree turn back to the bad in a heartbeat. It was nothing new.

Laura called with news regarding a phone conversation she had with someone at the Raleigh D.S.S. The hospital would be able to keep Tommy as long as he was listed as "acute." If and when he officially certified as Criterion Five, requiring residential care, the hospital would continue to treat him until other arrangements could be made. This was very reassuring to us. Any change in placement would have only exacerbated Tommy's violent behavior. At least the D.S.S. realized the need to protect my other children from Tommy. People were finally listening, slowly restoring my faith in the goodness of humanity.

One evening, Mark called Tommy and was informed that at around three that afternoon, Tommy had launched into a full-blown screaming tantrum. He had spent an hour kicking things, screaming and cursing at the staff. He accused them of doing things that they hadn't. The nurse on the phone asked us if we knew he had these kinds of fits. Taken aback by the question, Mark explained to her that was precisely why he was there in the first place.

Soon thereafter, Tommy began displaying delusional behavior. He thought he was Peter Pan, insisting we call him that on the phone. Tommy had been allowed to watch a popular movie about Peter Pan. When we asked if he was just pretending, he told us no, he was really Peter Pan and that he could really fly. When the staff at the hospital tried to convince him that he wasn't Peter Pan, he threw a screaming fit that lasted all afternoon. The staff member we spoke with that evening asked Mark if Tommy had ever fixated on characters before. Mark told them that these delusions were exactly the reason why we hadn't let him watch television in over two years. While we were aching because he was so sick, we rejoiced that others were seeing the full extent of what we had gone through. It would be the only way he could be truly helped; his doctors had to see firsthand what had terrified us for so very long.

A phone call came from Tommy the next evening. Tommy said he was on level one, the lowest behavioral rating, for his bad behavior. He said he had kicked another nurse that morning. He said, "I'm nervous about being called Tommy. It drives me nuts. I can't fly until I catch my shadow."

The next morning, we got a call from the nurse that Tommy had kicked. Dr. Frank wanted to put Tommy on Risperadal, a second anti-psychotic. I gave permission, but I was concerned about the use of two anti-psychotics together, something I had never heard of.

Tommy had to be isolated later that morning because of a tantrum he had after falling off a bicycle. Things seemed pretty dark: This poor nine-year-old needed two anti-psychotics as well as medication for aggression just to be somewhat functional. I wondered how we had been able to survive with Tommy on no medication at all for such a long time. It was taking a whole staff of people and four different medications to keep him quiet.

– c h a p t e r   f o u r t e e n –

Help Arrives

June 14th started like any other day, plagued with worry about Tommy. That afternoon the phone rang. A woman who said her name was Ms. Johnson was calling from the office of the state senator to whom I had written a letter. I could scarcely believe what I was hearing as the sympathetic woman told me how sorry they were to hear what we were going through and that they were already making phone calls to see what they could do to help us.

Tommy's case manager, Barbara, called me the next morning with an urgent request for Mark to come sign release forms for the senator's office. Hope that Tommy finally would get the help he desperately needed was starting to fill up my hope-deprived soul and it sure felt good.

That night around seven, Mark answered the phone and waved me over. It was Barbara asking to speak to us. My hands were shaking as I shared the receiver with Mark. She quickly informed us that she was calling with good news. Tommy had been certified for *Willie M.* that afternoon. The *Willie M.* program would monitor Tommy's treatment until the age of eighteen. Tommy would finally be guaranteed the level of services that he needed. We thanked Barbara profusely and hung up the phone.

All the heartache and struggle to get Tommy help had borne fruit. We had finally gotten him the aid that we had been afraid would never come. Our prayers had finally been answered.

We had all been through so much to get to this point, but we had all learned a lot, as well. We had learned about sexual abuse and its horrible effects on innocent children. We had learned volumes about mental illness and its devastating effects on family members. Mark and I had learned that our marriage was strong and that our family was the most important thing in the world to us. We had learned not to give up, but instead to keep fighting until we could rise above adversity. We knew absolutely that love is the strongest power. Real love holds you securely during the inevitable storms of life. I had personally learned that I could make things that I had viewed as impossible happen, if I just tried long and hard enough. Knowing that felt empowering to me. The fight to find help for Tommy had lasted over five years but I hadn't given up. The battle had served to strengthen me. Working together, the mental health professionals and I had finally found him the treatment he needed for his severe mental illness.

Of course, we all were aware this wasn't the end of Tommy's problems, but it was a new beginning for our family. We finally could know for sure that he would get the help he needed. We finally had a real chance to concentrate on helping our other children recover from the trauma Tommy had inflicted on them. It wasn't going to be easy, but I was looking forward to each moment we would spend together. We had all been so caught up in Tommy's pain for so long that we had forgotten how to have fun and enjoy each other.

We felt we had guardian angels watching over us, in the form of Tommy's new *Willie M.* case manager, Patty, and her boss, Dr. Riker. Meeting with Patty that day, it became apparent that she was experienced and totally dedicated to the cause of helping disturbed and violent children. Though extremely professional when speaking, her soft brown eyes indicated a very sensitive and kind person dwelling inside of her.

She asked for a detailed history of everything we had been through. For hours, I poured my heart out and she patiently listened. The reassurance she gave me that my continual need to make sure the other children would be kept safe from Tommy and that he would finally be treated was understood completely, providing much needed inner peace.

Just watching my children sitting, peacefully playing or watching television, I smiled knowing they were relaxed for the first time in so very long. Not hearing death threats accompanied by screamed curse words was something to be treasured each day. And each night, as we lay down to sleep, we were able to do just that, sleep.

Tommy was finally placed in residential care. He was admitted to the sexually reactive children's treatment program. There he began receiving intensive therapy. The program worked toward teaching Tommy to identify his inappropriate behaviors, hopefully redirecting him toward not re-offending.

Summer seemed to pass quickly into fall. Unfortunately, despite the therapy and medication, Tommy was still a very sick child. He had attacked the staff several times, continuing to throw fits with increased frequency. Going over the progress notes the hospital made in his records, I saw the definition of his different personalities. Dr. Frank had tried changing Tommy's meds but, so far, had seen no real signs of progress.

In November, a new psychologist, Dr. Gordon came into Tommy's life. At her request, I wrote a twelve-page letter that detailed his complete history, his behaviors and the nuances I'd noticed of each of his personalities. While I was not trying to diagnose Tommy or to influence her diagnosis, I wanted to inform her of everything I knew about my stepson, after more than five years of caring for him and loving him. Dr. Gordon took this plethora of information in and watched Tommy very carefully. She has acknowledged that treating him may be a lifetime process. It comforts me to know that she and Dr. Frank are working together. We are all working together, as a team, to help Tommy.

Mark and I know in our hearts that Tommy may never get better. We have grieved through this realization and accept it. Denying that he is sick wouldn't have gotten Tommy the help that he now has. Facing the painful truth is what got him help. Denial would have only prolonged the inevitable. We love our son, but know that we may never be able to live with him, because he is dangerous to himself and others. In my heart I truly believe, if given the opportunity, Tommy would kill someone and feel absolutely no remorse. Thanks to all the dedicated professionals now helping him, I no longer have terrors that I will be the mother of the student who guns down classmates at school. No longer do I imagine myself as the mother of a serial killer, watching her stepson face trial. By the grace of God, we were able to set in motion a probable lifelong process to prevent Tommy from ever becoming a killer or a rapist. It is my firm belief that hospitalizing Tommy is the only chance we have at preventing possible tragedy.

On his unit, Tommy has been rated as the one most likely to re-offend sexually. He probably will grow up in the hospital, a group home or a therapeutic foster home until the age of eighteen. We just don't see how we could ever trust him not to harm or sexually molest our other children. Mark and I are not willing to put them at risk of harm, never again. They have a right to grow up safe in their own home. They have a right to be protected. In society, the rules are set up to protect the majority. My home will have to be that way, too. Jeff, Kyle, Jessica, Bobby, Jake, Megan and Kristen are the majority and they must be protected from Tommy, even if he is family.

We are so very grateful that our state watches over the care of violent children. It is my sincerest hope that they will continue to do so. If they do, my children and others will grow up safe and Tommy will be kept from hurting himself. Not getting him help undoubtedly would have meant a lifetime of swimming in the judicial system. Being in the hospital insures that those who may have been his potential victims will not be harmed.

part two

The Power
of Positive Advocacy

– c h a p t e r   o n e –

Becoming an Advocate

O ne of the hardest crises a parent can face is to learn that their child suffers from mental illness. All of a sudden, the world seems to turn upside down, leaving you confused about what to do to help your child. To compound this, navigating the mental healthcare system can seem like trying to slay a dragon with a toothpick. You are not quite sure what to do, or how to do it, which may leave you feeling helpless and alone. Trying to figure out how to get appropriate help for your child can seem overwhelming and even frightening. Where do you begin? Who do you call? How do you communicate the needs of your child and get the services you think he or she needs?

Realizing that you need help for your child and that it is up to you to find it is the starting point from which you begin the journey of becoming an advocate for your child. While mental illness in a child can be a difficult reality to face, denial of the problem will only prolong the inevitable need for professional help. Congratulate yourself on being able to recognize that your child needs the expert help of mental health professionals. You have just taken your first step in helping your child. The road ahead will probably be long and hard, but with the right attitude, you can survive this crisis successfully with a minimum of frustration, anxiety and headache.

Finding appropriate services for a mentally ill child often depends solely on the advocacy efforts of the parent. An advocate is essentially someone who acts as the "voice" of the child and ideally is a person who has intimate knowledge of the child and his or her needs. Children who suffer from mental illnesses cannot speak for themselves and so need the kinds of support advocates provide: pulling together mental healthcare professionals and appropriate services. In short, an advocate represents the child when dealing with the mental healthcare system and makes sure the child's needs are appropriately met. Advocacy may sound like a daunting task, but the remainder of this book will show you positive methods that facilitate the process of getting help for your mentally ill child. This second part will take the mystery out of the mental healthcare system, allowing you to navigate it effectively, with greater confidence and ease.

An important part of becoming an effective advocate is realizing that you are not alone in trying to help the child. As I am sure you may already know from experience, loneliness is an emotion that seems to be a part of having a mentally ill child or family member. Parents of the mentally ill often feel extreme isolation and even embarrassment, because of the unusual and often overwhelming problems they face. Sometimes, we even feel guilty, because our loved one is ill. We love the child but, in all honesty, we hate the illness and the effects it has on the youngster and everyone in the family. I know all about these feelings, firsthand.

Shortly after Tommy and Bobby came to live with us, my journey as an advocate began. The road was very long for us and sometimes frustrating. I have spent many nights lying awake trying to think of effective ways to help my stepsons. Through the last few years, I have tried many different methods of advocacy—some that worked and some that failed. In this part of the book, we will discuss why some methods work especially well and why some are doomed to failure. Trial and error was the best teacher I had when it came to developing my methods of positive advocacy. I had to experience failure, re-evaluate the situation and find a better method. Through it all, I grew into a much stronger person, and looking back, the experiences, both good and bad, taught me a great deal.

Positive advocacy will help you learn to communicate with mental health professionals effectively and develop teamwork skills to eradicate problems caused by even the most severe disorders. With doctors, mental health professionals, school systems, and parent/advocates working together as a team to help the child, the chances of successful treatment greatly increase.

There are, unfortunately, thousands of parents like my husband and myself who have mentally ill children. That there are others who suffer the pain we have felt may help us feel less isolated, but at the same time it leaves us saddened that other parents experience the very same pain we feel, day after day. Nevertheless, we all have a valuable asset. There are mental healthcare professionals who, when we locate them, will help us, because they have dedicated themselves to the cause of helping mentally ill children. Though you may have to search for the right professional for your child, when you find him or her, the person will provide the help your mentally ill child needs.

Persist. You are not alone.

chapter two

Taking the First Step

Parents of mentally ill children face unique problems and challenges every day. The list of troubles is endless. We feel sadness that our child is suffering. We feel an overwhelming sense of powerlessness and loss of control. We miss the way things used to be. We feel envious that our friends and relatives have "normal" children, and wish our child could be "normal" again too. We get frustrated with friends and family members who don't know what to say to us or how to help us. All of these emotions create a feeling of distance from those we care about, leaving parents of mentally ill children feeling isolated, helpless and alone.

Let's review some of the pressures with which the family of a mentally ill child is often faced. Please be aware that most of the problems I will discuss are worst-case scenarios, but I feel it is important for those dealing with severely mentally ill children to have someone be honest with them about what handling the problem can really entail.

Having a mentally ill child often puts a tremendous strain on a marriage. The couple can quickly find that their lives center on the mentally ill child, leaving no time for one another. Mark and I would often take a break and go out to dinner alone and somehow always find the conversation revolving around Tommy. Even when we made a concerted effort not to talk about him, somehow things always turned back to that subject. We began to lose touch as a couple and to feel isolated from each other. Mark was involved in his work and I shouldered the responsibilities of the children. I often took Tommy and Bobby to their various appointments with doctors alone. I needed Mark to be there and he was, when work permitted, but most of the time it was just me. Sometimes, I felt resentful when Mark could escape the problems at home and go to work. Little did I realize, he spent all his time at work worrying and dreading every ring of the telephone for fear of receiving disturbing news. There would be times when he didn't want to talk about Tommy's illness but I needed to. I would be hurt that he wouldn't talk and he would be mad that I was pushing him to talk. This was the first time in our marriage that we had ever felt distance between us and it was scary. We were two people who loved each other very much and were trying to cope with an overwhelming problem.

Another issue is the financial pressure that can build because of the child's illness. Suddenly, the family has to deal with the ongoing expenses of treatment, medications, etcetera. Often, mothers and fathers must take time off from work to take the child for treatment, sometimes several times a week. Job pressures may increase due to these absences. Often, bosses fail to understand the need for such absences from work and this can jeopardize the parent's job status.

Other children in the family often suffer because of the mentally ill child and the constant attention that the parents must give to the situation. Some children tend to withdraw from the family as a way of dealing with their stress, other children may begin to act out to get their parent's attention. Then not only do the harried parents have to deal with the problems of their mentally ill child, but they must deal with the other children's problems on top of it. I used to compare it to being caught in a cyclone. The world seemed to be ripping apart around us and all I could do was wonder how to stop the tornado that was tearing our family apart. Parents often feel stretched to their economic and emotional limit, trying hard to help their mentally ill child and still give necessary attention to the other children in the family. Add to this mix financial pressure and marital problems and it can be enough to make even the strongest person throw up his hands and say "I give up!"

As I said before, you must realize that help is out there. Trust me. I am living proof that you can find it. The first step to breaking the cycle of pain that you are experiencing is reaching out for help for your mentally ill loved one, and to do that you simply have to dedicate yourself to that cause. As parents, we have already dedicated ourselves to these human beings we call our children. Advocating for them is really a natural extension of that dedication.

The goal of advocating for your mentally ill child is to get them as much help as possible with the best possible outcome. Luckily, there are many places to turn to for help with your mentally ill child and your family. There are therapists, psychologists, psychiatrists, social workers, school guidance counselors and primary care physicians. Help may also be sought through private practitioners or from the local mental health agency. One thing to be aware of is that while only physicians and psychiatrists are able to prescribe medications for psychiatric illness, other professionals are usually willing to refer you to a doctor who can provide medication should the need arise during therapy. In many cases, a combination of medication and therapy is the most effective course of action.

Ironically, reaching out for help can sometimes be the hardest step of all. I remember sometimes feeling like a rat lost in a maze during our journey through the mental healthcare system. I felt embarrassed telling complete strangers about the serious problem that was going on in my home. I guess I thought that they wouldn't believe such a bizarre story. After all, I had trouble believing the way Tommy and Bobby were acting. Luckily, there are therapists and psychiatrists who are not judgmental and are compassionate listeners and really want to help. Helping your child will be their goal. I learned that, for most of them, their jobs weren't just jobs, but a passion that stemmed from their hearts.

Trust me, when you make that first call to a therapist, admitting to yourself your child has a serious problem, you will feel relief. Making the decision that you cannot help your child yourself and your child needs professional help can be heart wrenching, but it is the right thing to do. You are doing what is best for your son or daughter, no matter how much it hurts. Make the call, get an appointment, see a professional, start to take positive steps! You will be glad you did!

A Note from Dr. Pastore: *"As parents and professionals, we create safe, holding environments for our children to help them grow. When a child is mentally ill, we need **more** hands to help create safety and holding."*

– *c h a p t e r   t h r e e* –

The Advocate's Responsibilities

By making an appointment for your child to see a mental healthcare professional, you have taken the first step in becoming your child's advocate. On the initial visit to your chosen professional, make sure you give the person a complete and accurate history of your child. This history is very important in determining what problems your child may have and why he or she may be having them. Relaying personal information about your family may be difficult, but withholding information could delay diagnosis and hinder treatment. Because children are often unable to effectively communicate exactly what is wrong, professionals have to take information from several sources to put together a complete picture of the child's behavioral problems and parents are usually the primary source.

Keep a Journal Detailing your Child's Behaviors
Keeping an accurate journal is a very effective way to document behavioral problems. Take your journal to your child's first mental health appointment and every appointment thereafter. What may seem like an incident of little importance to you may in fact be vital information that

could lead to a more complete diagnosis. If your child's mental health-care professionals asks to read the journal, let them do so. Don't be embarrassed or afraid that a counselor or physician will use what you have written to judge you. The professional is looking for any clue or pattern as to why your child has been acting out in frightening ways.

Open up and tell your child's professional the intimate details of what is going on. Don't try to sugarcoat it. You are there because you and your child need help. In order for your child to obtain the help he needs, the professional must be told exactly what the child is doing so he or she can diagnose and treat the child. Mental healthcare professionals understand the turmoil you are going through and think that parents who seek help for their children are making the best choice. They know that great amounts of love have impacted the decision and that it is often hard for a family to admit that there is a problem. Good mental health professionals will go to great lengths to be friendly and put the family at ease.

Write Your Questions Down

It is a good idea to write down everything you want to ask the mental health professional before your first visit and before each subsequent visit. Doing so will insure that you remember the questions that come up. Writing down the answers to your questions and ideas the professional has about treating your child is also helpful. You can review these notes later, if you need to. I found keeping track of the therapist's advice especially helpful. I could go home and study my notes when things quieted down at night; reviewing and generating ideas. This helped me to form my personal plan to implement the therapist's suggestions into our daily routine.

Often, getting a child correctly diagnosed and treated may seem like a rather slow process to a family in pain. However, be aware the professional may need time to gather information about your child from such sources as past medical and school records before he or she feels that an accurate diagnosis and treatment plan can be outlined. This may seem frustrating, but it is important to realize that the person treating your child is being thorough. Do everything you can to expedite and facilitate the information-gathering process.

Do Your Own Research

Accessing and gaining more information about your child's condition will help you to feel more in control of the situation. When Tommy was first diagnosed with schizophrenia, I spent hours at the local library poring over medical books searching for every smidgen of information I could find on the subject. Doing so made it easier for me to ask informed questions and voice concerns I had about his care and the medications he was taking. Most of Tommy's therapists appreciated the fact that I wanted to learn all I could about his mental illness. I was able to ask intelligent questions about his treatment, discuss treatment options that I had read about and express concerns that my research had brought to my attention. Occasionally, I even brought up something that the psychiatrist had not yet read about. He or she would also look up the information that I had brought to their attention so that we could discuss it the following week. Together, we would decide if the new information would be helpful to Tommy's treatment plan. Research makes you a proactive part of the team.

The Internet is a good place to begin. There are a plethora of websites on just about every mental illness and most medications. Some have research studies on mental illness and give you the names of support groups as well. When you surf the net for information, you will find stories of others going through what you are going through and these can provide comfort and possibly new insights and suggestions for coping with your child's illness. Always do backup research as well to be sure the information on the web is correct.

Communicate with Your Child's Mental Health Professional

Open communication with the therapist or physician is one of the most important things to have in order to help your child. If you feel that the person is not answering your questions fully, tell him or her.

One of the biggest complaints that parents of mentally ill children have is that their children's professional can seem distant or preoccupied at times. This can be very troublesome for parents to deal with. Understanding that these people may be overwhelmed with a staggering caseload is important. While your case undoubtedly is important to the worker, the person may have more urgent or pressing issues regarding another case, but professional confidentiality prevents him or her from discussing other cases with you. It is impossible for the mental healthcare provider to tell you if another case is causing pressure or taking up much of the individual's time.

If you feel like your child's professional seems distant or seems to have his or her attention elsewhere, tell the person your concerns and listen to their reply since they may be unaware of what you are feeling. Whatever you do, don't keep your feelings about this subject to yourself.

Hopefully, if you have a problem with your child's therapist, you will choose to tell the person about it. If you do, make sure it is done in a straightforward and non-confrontational manner. Yelling and screaming will only serve to strain, or even shut down, the communication between you and your child's professional. Having your child see you get upset with his or her therapist may even affect your child's ability to trust the mental health professional. Think carefully about how to best approach the professional, especially if your child is present. A parent's positive attitude can set a shining example for the child.

What If You Can't Seem to Communicate?

If you come across a therapist or doctor who seems unconcerned about your needs as a parent, remind the person that as the parent of a mentally ill child, you have a right to be included in every aspect of your child's treatment. This is not to say that your child's professional shouldn't have private sessions alone with your child. Most therapy sessions are set up so that the professional talks alone with your child, and afterwards the parents are invited in to discuss their concerns. This is normal procedure. You should, however, be aware of what methods are used to treat your child and kept up to date on the professionals concerns for your child and any progress your child is making. You and your healthcare professional should be working together as a team, for the good of the child. If your healthcare professional doesn't take a team approach, it may be time to find a new caregiver.

Fortunately, I have experienced inadequate care for my stepson only rarely, but, when you recognize substandard care, remove your child from it immediately. You must often follow your gut instinct when it comes to the best care and treatment for your child's illness. If, after careful consideration, you feel that your child isn't getting the best possible care for his illness, find care elsewhere. We never regretted putting Tommy back into the outpatient care of a psychiatrist we trusted instead of keeping him hospitalized in the care of a psychologist we didn't. Making the decision to pull him out of a hospital was something we agonized over and, admittedly, were even a little afraid to do. In the end, we realized that what we felt in our hearts was in Tommy's best interest and was the right thing to do.

Now that you are aware of the tools you will need to be a successful advocate, we can begin to discuss the other ways you can be the best advocate for your mentally ill child.

Primary Responsibilities of an Advocate

- Recognize that the child is in need of professional help.
- Choose and enlist the help of mental healthcare professionals.
- Provide professionals with a detailed history of the child.
- Provide professionals with all relevant current information on the child.
- Keep a journal of the child's behaviors.
- Make lists of questions and concerns for your child's professional.
- Write down answers to your questions/advice from professional.
- Give child prescribed medications as directed
- Schedule and keep appointments with mental health providers.
- Research your child's illness so that you can ask informed questions regarding treatment options.
- Follow the suggested treatment recommendations carefully and thoroughly.
- Call a professional immediately if you suspect your child is in crisis!

Turn Your Anger Into Action

- Whenever you feel yourself overwhelmed with angry feelings, take time-out and recognize what you are feeling. Release pent-up frustration in positive ways, such as physical exercise or even a good cry. These actions may help to clear your mind. Once the physical frustration is released, begin focusing on the problem.
- Assess the situation; review what has made you feel angry and think of positive ways in which you could take action to improve your child's situation.

- Formulate a plan of action. Often, this plan will begin to make you feel more in control of an upsetting situation.
- Doing something positive about your problem will make you feel better. Energy that would have been wasted on feeling angry is now channeled into taking action, a positive energy force. This positive force becomes your internal energy, necessary to propel you toward finding a solution for your problem. Take action! Often something as simple as making a phone call to someone who may be able to help you can restore your feelings of hope.

– c h a p t e r   f o u r –

In the Therapist's Office

In most professional offices, there is the dreaded waiting room. Dealing with a mentally ill child can make this time even more difficult. Mental healthcare professionals usually keep their appointments in a timely manner, follow a strict half-hour to an hour booking schedule and end their sessions based on the clock. This is different from a typical doctor's visit where you may spend an hour or more waiting if the doctor's schedule gets backed up. I always appreciated the fact that Tommy's appointments began right on time. But bear in mind that there are occasional emergency situations that demand the professional's attention and may make the appointment begin late. Try to be patient if your child's professional is helping a patient in crisis. Remember, someday it could be your child who needs the professional's extra attention. It should make you feel satisfied to know that if your own child was experiencing a crisis, his or her doctors would take the time necessary to help.

You will need to arrive a little early for your first appointment. There will be paperwork that you will need to fill out that requires your insurance card, so be sure to bring it. Also, don't forget to bring your journal and questions you've written down for the first visit. There will probably be brief questions about the child's history on the forms. Answer these as honestly as you can.

Most mental healthcare professionals have very comfortable offices, which often are stocked with toys for children to play with. The professionals will introduce themselves to you and your child. Don't be surprised if they get down on the floor when they introduce themselves to your child. By putting themselves at eye level with the child, they establish a mutual comfort. I still fondly remember one of Tommy's psychiatrists, dressed in an expensive wool skirt and jacket, getting right down on the floor and playing with the children during their therapy. I found that quite endearing and liked the fact that she was so comfortable with children. By getting down on their level, she ensured that the children trusted her and were more open to talking to her about what had happened to them.

The first visit usually begins with the parents giving the professional a complete rundown of the child's history and current behavior problems. The parents will tell the professional what is going on with the child, state their concerns and then be asked to leave the office and return to the waiting room. Parents need to understand that the professional needs time alone with the child to assess the child's behavior, and allow them to open up about their own feelings. Sometimes, with his or her parents in the room, the child will say things that he thinks will please the parents. Once the parents leave, the professional can see how the child acts when free from parental supervision.

What are they doing in there? Good question! The professionals, whether therapists, psychiatrists or social workers, will probably sit right down on the floor and try to talk with your child. They will try to make the child as comfortable as possible by not pushing the child too hard to interact with them. Sometimes, they will just observe the child playing alone. Eventually, the child will get to know the professionals and open up to them about his or her feelings, usually while playing with toys. This is called "play therapy." Mental health professionals can actually tell a lot about a child by how he or she interacts with toys, such as dolls. Just sit and watch your own child play with a doll sometime. Does he or she cuddle it? Pretend to feed it? Comfort it? That's a very good sign. In Tommy's case, he would take the doll over to the play sink and pretend to drown it, a reenactment of what he saw his mother's boyfriend do to Bobby.

After a while, the professionals will return to the waiting rooms and ask the parents to return to the sessions. They will then tell the parents their assessments of the situation and what they think is wrong. Don't expect the professionals to come up with a diagnosis after just one visit. Allow the professional to take time to thoroughly gather all the information they need in order to make a diagnosis. They may be able to offer a preliminary diagnosis, or even several possible ones on the first visit, but if they don't, try not to panic. Taking time to make a firm diagnosis is a sign of a good therapist. Suppose your child had a mild disorder, and they prescribed medication for a severe disorder. You wouldn't want that! Be patient. Diagnosis can take weeks or even months to formulate. Let the professionals do their jobs and take their time to formulate educated opinions of what is wrong with your child.

The professionals will probably give you some suggestions of methods you may try at home to help with your child's behavioral problems. Be sure and write these down. Sometimes, they may seem a little bit silly, but through personal experience, I have seen some of these methods work. At the very least, give the professionals' suggested methods a reasonable try. Some of these methods may include: keeping behavior charts, rewards for positive behaviors, positive reinforcement methods and even ignoring certain behaviors to stop the pattern of a child getting too much attention for negative behaviors. Don't feel insulted if they suggest you handle your child in new and different ways. Their experience and expertise is why you've consulted these people. Their methods will work. Something as simple as changing the way you react to your child can have a very positive effect on your child's behaviors.

When you leave a professional's office for the first time, you may notice something different about yourself. You may feel as if a huge burden has been lifted off your shoulders. Mark and I certainly did. Taking Tommy and Bobby to a therapist for the first time made us feel much better. We knew that we were doing the right thing and that we were on the right track. We now had someone to help us carry the heavy load that our hearts were bearing and we knew we were getting help for the boys. When we left their therapist's office that afternoon, we were actually smiling. We knew we now had some help.

The Keys to Positive Advocacy

1. Recognize that your child needs professional help and find the best assistance available for him or her.
2. Take your responsibilities as an advocate seriously and follow through with them.
3. Turn feelings of anger and frustration into positive energy.
4. Speak from the heart to those you are asking to help your mentally ill child.
5. Focus on teamwork between yourself, the schools and any professional helping your child.
6. Be patient when it comes to treatment, medication and duration of treatment. Have a patient attitude towards those professionals and educators trying to help your child.
7. Always show kindness, respect and gratitude toward those striving to provide help for your child.
8. Stay focused on the goal of helping your mentally ill child.
9. Take care of yourself, so that you can continue to be an effective, positive advocate.

—chapter five—

Treatment Options

There are many different options when it comes to the treatment of mental illness. Sometimes your child's mental healthcare provider will recommend a combination of two or more methods. This is not uncommon and can be quite effective. Because everyone is different and will respond differently to treatment options, individuals require treatment plans tailored to their own specific needs. This will be the job of your child's designated mental healthcare professional, who in effect is relying on the input and help of the parent/advocate. A plan of treatment will be designed for your child and changed accordingly as your child's needs change over time. Let's explore a few of these options.

Therapy

Therapy can occur in an individual setting or in a group setting, and usually involves talking to the child about his or her problems and implementing various methods of allowing the child to work through his or her feelings. Therapy techniques are wide-ranging and varied and can differ in type from drawing pictures, role-playing, using puppets to communicate inner-feelings, behavioral modification or many other interesting, well-researched techniques. Don't forget to ask questions about the treatment methods, why they were assigned or why they may not be working. Your child's therapist should be happy to explain them to you and provide reassurance as to why he or she chose those therapy techniques for your child. Remember, doing research on your own regarding therapeutic techniques may help to alleviate any concerns you may have or may open up the lines of communication regarding other therapies.

When asked to participate in your child's therapy session, do so willingly. This will send your child the message that you really care about helping him or her. It is important for the mentally ill child to see that his or her parents are supportive of what the mental health professional is doing. An important factor in the success of any kind of therapy is that the patient trust his mental health professional. Seeing his or her parents demonstrate their trust in the professional through their inclusion and participation in the therapy session, further reinforces the feelings of trust the child has for the professional. Your participation in therapy, when invited to do so, can do a lot to help your child.

Some Qualities of a Good Mental Health Professional

- She takes the time to address your concerns about your child.
- He always gets a thorough history on the child, including information from the patient's school.
- She takes the time to answer any questions you may have about your child's treatment plan.
- He addresses your concerns about medication, including discussing any possible side effects that you may need to be aware of.
- She returns your calls promptly if you have a question or concern about your child.
- He makes you feel like part of the team that is helping the child and does not treat you as if you were an outsider.
- She doesn't negate your feelings, rather, she addresses them with you.
- If he isn't able to find answers as to what is wrong with your child, a good professional either enlists the help of other qualified mental healthcare professionals, or makes an appropriate referral to someone considered to be more qualified to treat your child's illness.

- She indicates empathy for you as a parent. In my opinion, that's one of the very best qualities of a good mental health professional.

Medication

Medication can be extremely helpful in treating some forms of mental illness. The thought of putting children on medication sometimes frightens and upsets parents. I must admit, I was quite concerned the first time someone recommended medication for Tommy. To reassure myself that we were doing the right thing, I researched the illness with which he had been diagnosed and the treatments available. What I learned in my research allowed me to ask pertinent questions about the medication and its side effects and gave me confidence in the decisions I made.

Some mental illnesses are thought to be caused by chemical imbalances in the brain. Current research indicates depression, panic disorders, obsessive-compulsive disorders, anxiety disorders and many other illnesses may be caused in part or totally by these imbalances. Some doctors consider tendencies toward these chemical imbalances to be hereditary. Proper doses of medications, used to treat the symptoms of these illnesses, can help some patients a lot. Sometimes, because of medication, patients can live more normal lives, helping them to regain their self-esteem by keeping their symptoms under control.

One very important thing to note about medication is that it may take time to find just the right medication or combination of medicines to help your child. We all have a different body chemistry. That difference in body chemistry can be the reason that two people with the same kind of problem will react differently to the same medication. One child may do well on a certain medication and another might have no reaction at all or even a bad reaction. It takes time to try different medications until you find just the right one and just the right dosage, so be patient and follow the advice of your child's doctor. But don't be afraid to ask questions and communicate your child's behavior while on a drug.

Side effects are a serious concern for parents. Although this is quite rare, some of the stronger psychiatric medications can have dangerous or permanent side effects. Always ask your child's mental health professional about the possible side effects of any new medication your child may be about to try. If you notice some unusual reaction in your child that may be a side effect of the medication he or she is taking, report it to your child's professional immediately. By doing so, you can discuss what action, if any, you should take concerning continuing the medication. While it is good to know the side effects of medication your child is taking, don't let that knowledge lead to fear.

When treating some forms of psychiatric illness, some children may need as many as three or more medications to get their symptoms under control. It may seem frightening to think about giving your child several different medications at once, but current research has shown certain medications work well in combination with others. Often, the results of medication combination can be amazing when it comes to the treatment of mental illness. Psychiatrists tend to introduce the combination of medications into the child's system slowly, so that any adverse effects can be monitored. Medications are usually started one at a time and at very low doses for about a week or two. The dose is then increased for another week or so, and if necessary, may be increased again for a period of time until the desired effect has been obtained. Your child's doctor or psychiatrist will determine the rate at which the dosage will be adjusted. It is extremely important that you follow your physician's instructions about increasing dosages exactly as they have been dictated and indicate to him or her any adverse effects.

Do not raise the doses of medication your child is taking without first getting the advice and permission of the psychiatrist or medical doctor who has been treating your child. Also, be aware that certain over-the-counter medications may not mix well with prescription medications, particularly psychiatric medications. Always consult your child's doctor before giving him or her anything over-the-counter or any medication that your child's doctor may not be aware of that has been prescribed by another physician. Always keep all of the doctors, if your child sees more than one, apprised as to what medications he or she is taking. This can prevent accidental, dangerous drug interactions. As your child's advocate, it is your responsibility to make sure that each of your child's practitioners knows what the others have prescribed.

If a psychiatrist feels that a certain medication is not working for your child, he or she will usually wean him off it. Weaning means to slowly decrease the dosage over several days, or even weeks, until the child is safely withdrawn from the drug. This procedure is done slowly, for the child's safety, when a medication seems to be ineffective. Why not just stop administering the medication "cold turkey?" Because serious consequences may result if certain medications are withdrawn too quickly. For example, a dangerous increase in the child's blood pressure is possible. Not all medications prescribed for mental illness cause such problems if stopped too quickly, but only qualified psychiatric professionals or medical doctors know which ones might. Follow any advice about weaning your child exactly as you are told to do it. Never take your child off medication without first consulting his or her mental healthcare provider or medical doctor!

Psychiatrists take the medication they prescribe to children very seriously, as do the parents of mentally ill children. They are trying to find a way to help the child, not cause more problems. Good psychiatrists will listen to all of your concerns about medication and do their best to help you understand how the prescribed drugs are supposed to help your child, as well as talk to you about side effects. Ask questions!

It's extremely important to note that medication for psychiatric illness must be given consistently! This means giving the child the correct dosage and most importantly, giving the dosage at the correct time. If you have trouble remembering to give your child medications, three methods may help you remember to do so. One is to make a medication chart and put it on the refrigerator door and check off the time each medication is given that day. This way you can insure you haven't forgotten to administer a dose to your child. Another way you can insure giving the right medicine at the right time is to buy a watch with an alarm. Set the alarm to the dosage time for your child's medication. This should help you remember to give the child the medication on time; just don't forget to always wear the watch. Another very effective method is to buy a pillbox marked for morning, noon, evening, and bedtime (or something similar). This way you can put a day's worth of pills into the compartments the night before. If you have forgotten to give your child a dose of medication, you will know, because it is still in the compartment. As your child's parent/advocate, you are the one responsible for seeing that your child takes his medication properly. Proper dosing and timing of the dose can make all the difference in how your child reacts to the medication. By doing your part to see that your child takes the proper amount of medication and takes it on time, you are helping your child's progress toward getting better.

A Word About Friendly Advice

Parents often find themselves bombarded with advice from family members, grandparents, friends or even well meaning teachers. Sometimes, people you only talk to in passing will offer unsolicited advice. This advice can put parents under a lot of pressure, because it can cause confusion when trying to make the best treatment decisions for your child. Comments from others, can make you doubt yourself, your child's professional help and your child's treatment. Mark and I experienced this many times when it came to treatment for Tommy. My mother had one opinion, Mark's mother had another, my father had a different take on the situation altogether, the boy's maternal grandparents had their own ideas and friends often put in their two cents worth as well. Sometimes, Mark and I just didn't know which way to turn. Eventually, I learned that we had to get professional recommendations on treatment. Decisions were always best made between Mark, myself and Tommy's qualified mental health professional. The bottom line is it's your child who needs help and you have to make the decisions.

Discussing your feelings of confusion with your child's mental healthcare provider is always wise. He or she can help to alleviate the state of uncertainty you may be feeling, point out what's positive and negative about the options you are considering and explain why certain options are appropriate for your child. Don't worry about offending the provider by questioning treatment options. The majority of professionals will be glad that you are being open and honest with them about your concerns regarding treatment. Many will welcome such discussions, because this gives them the chance to further educate you about your child's needs. However, if you still feel apprehensive after discussing your concerns with your child's current mental healthcare provider, solicit a second opinion from another professional. This is a perfectly acceptable option—it's your child; you want the best care for him or her. A top-notch mental healthcare professional will not be offended if you seek a second opinion and in many cases, he or she will welcome it in order to support whatever decision you make regarding your child's treatment. They understand that your actions are out of love for your mentally ill child.

So, how do you handle the well-intentioned advice of outsiders? Always thank them for their concern for your child. In most cases, they only offer the advice because they care about the child. As such, a polite response is much preferred to getting upset. Answer the unsolicited comments of others with something such as, "Thank you for your concern for my child. I'll consider what you have said." This type of response shows gratitude for the show of concern and leaves the person who gave the advice feeling as though what they said was at least valid enough for you to consider. Of course, you don't have to take their advice or even consider it, but this way you aren't leaving them feeling badly or yourself feeling guilty for having given them a rude or sarcastic response. Using positive methods to respond to the suggestions will make you feel better about yourself.

Hospitalization

The thought of committing a child to a psychiatric hospital strikes fear into the hearts of most parents. Facing the fact that your child's illness is not controllable with medication and outpatient therapy and that the child needs more intense treatment is very difficult. I know this feeling from personal experience. Tommy was five when we first had to make the decision to hospitalize him because of his violent behavior. He had attempted to stab my daughter with a pair of scissors.

When in the throes of his anger, Tommy had almost superhuman strength. I was no match for it and neither were the other children. He once lifted his 220-pound father off the ground during one of his fits and another time badly injured my arm. Frankly, as time went on and we learned the extent of his rage, we all were terrified of this child. None of us slept soundly. We always were afraid he would hurt or kill us in our sleep. Our lives revolved around keeping the other children safe from Tommy. Tommy needed more help than just therapy twice a week and the several medications he was taking. We had to quit denying the severity of his mental illness and hoping that someday he was going to magically just get better. We finally had to face the most painful decision that the parent of a mentally ill child has to make. Tommy needed to be hospitalized immediately!

I learned the hard way that while love can help a lot of problems, when it comes to mental illness, you need the help of professionals. Love cannot overcome a chemical imbalance or serious emotional problems. With the help of trained professionals, therapy, medication and sometimes even hospitalization, the sick child will get the help he or she needs. It's a hard fact to face, but sometimes loving someone isn't enough to bring about healing. Sometimes, loving someone with mental illness means that you have to make hard decisions when it comes to helping them. Hospitalizing Tommy was the hardest decision our family ever made, and as it turned out, one of the best.

Psychiatric hospitals are usually set up with a system of rules that the patients are required to follow. Discipline may be implemented for unsafe behaviors. Usually, there is a quiet room, used to seclude children throwing tantrums. Secluding them allows them to safely vent their anger and take time to calm down. Restraints are rarely used anymore, only in worst-case scenarios where a patient is psychotic and completely beyond control. Today's mental hospitals strive to treat their patients in the least-restrictive environment possible. Patients usually earn privileges for cooperative behavior. This method encourages young patients to strive for better behavior, because they are rewarded for it. Positive motivation can be effective in children.

Patients in the hospital receive intensive therapy during their stays. There are private sessions with psychiatrists, usually at least once a day. They may also be under the care of psychologists during their hospitalizations. Therapy may be done privately or in group sessions. Patients are required to attend most of these sessions. Sometimes, as Tommy did, they refuse to go to therapy and thus lose privileges because of their defiant behavior.

Family members are allowed to visit, usually during certain hours and sometimes only on certain days of the week. Phone calls may be restricted, because these are usually considered privileges and, in most cases, have to be earned by the patient as a reward for good behavior. Restricted visitation may seem upsetting to parents, but remember, your child is there to get better. Sometimes having the patient away from the home and family allows the hospital professionals to observe a child's true mental state more clearly. Tommy was always known for having what they called a "honeymoon period." He would be very good for a few days and then suddenly, he would explode into a tirade that caused one social worker to remark to Tommy's psychiatrist, "He is the sickest child I have ever seen." In one episode, Tommy had thrown himself around his hospital room for forty-five minutes straight, bruising himself all over his body. Had he not been in a hospital environment for several days, his doctors might not have known just how violent he could become. By observing a child over time, doctors often can see behaviors in a child that an outpatient psychiatrist probably wouldn't discover by talking to the child for just an hour or two per week. I remember actually feeling a sense of relief when the doctors at the hospital finally saw Tommy violently acting out as I had been reporting to his psychiatrist for the last year. Children who have behavior problems are usually only capable of controlling them for so long, and sooner or later they let their problems show. Hospitalization is often the best chance for a doctor to truly assess what is wrong with the child. Even if your child is prone to "honeymoon periods" like Tommy, don't worry, hospital psychiatrists are well aware that some children are very good at hiding their behavioral problems at first. An experienced doctor will be able to see past the child's façade of perfect behavior.

Having the opportunity to observe the child in the hospital twenty-four hours a day can help the professionals get a better handle on the diagnosis of a severely mentally ill child. It took two consecutive hospitalizations before Tommy was finally diagnosed as schizophrenic with homicidal and suicidal tendencies and suffering from post-traumatic stress disorder. Needless to say, Tommy had many severe psychiatric problems that would need extensive treatment, probably over his lifetime. The hospital psychiatrist was only able to diagnose Tommy so accurately because he had several days to observe him day and night. Tommy's regular psychiatrist was also grateful for the diagnosis made by her colleague. She trusted his professional judgment and when Tommy was released, she was able to prescribe medications more suited to his illness and restructure his therapy to address the new diagnosis.

Hospitalizations are usually short, generally due to stringent financial restrictions placed on doctors and medical facilities by insurance companies. Insurance companies have essentially tied the hands of hospital mental healthcare professionals when it comes to length of stay.

Doctors can and do request more days of hospitalization for patients whom they feel they need more time to help. It all boils down to whether the insurance companies approve the additional stays or not. If they do not and the patients don't have additional sources of funding, then, much to the disappointment of the doctors treating them at the hospitals, the patients are discharged. Unfortunately, the insurance companies are the one paying the hospital bills, so hospitals have no other choice but to comply. This is a frustrating glitch in the mental healthcare system that needs correction. The government could easily pass a law requiring insurance companies to provide the same level of care to the mentally ill as they do to the physically ill, but insurance companies say that if that happens, their rates for all clients will skyrocket. Mental health advocacy groups have been trying to get this disparity resolved for years, but so far, very little has been accomplished.

Patients are usually discharged into the care of their previous mental healthcare professionals, so that therapy and treatment can continue after hospitalization.

Occasionally, a child like Tommy will not respond well to limited inpatient treatment and residential care will be recommended. This can last anywhere from a few months to several years, depending on the child's progress. While this definitely is not a recommendation a parent wants to hear, sometimes there is no other choice. Know that if this is recommended, your child needs intensive therapy and psychiatric treatment he or she cannot obtain while in your home or during a short hospital stay.

Guilt is an emotion that parents often feel when committing their child to long-term care. It is important to realize that loving a child sometimes means that you have to make painfully hard decisions that are best for the child. Residential care can do a lot to help severely mentally ill children that a lesser level of care would not. Parents of a child suffering from severe mental illness often have no other choice but residential care, for the safety and welfare of their mentally ill child and the protection of their other children.

Our son Tommy is currently in residential care at a group home. Tommy receives therapy sessions to address his problems, a psychiatrist to monitor medication and special education services. He lives in a very structured environment. The staff is comprised of dedicated indi-

viduals who are highly trained to handle children with severe emotional and mental problems.

After his first few hospitalizations proved to be of limited help,
there were no hospitals left in the state in which we lived that could
treat a child like Tommy, who sexually molested other children. That is
why we decided Tommy could no longer live in our home. This was
probably the hardest thing with which Mark and I ever had to deal. Our
hearts ached about this decision and we still find ourselves feeling sad.
There was just no other alternative left, though, and we had to accept
that Tommy needed to go, even though at times it felt like our hearts
were going to literally shatter. Tommy hasn't made a lot of progress
since going into residential care, but there have been small signs of
improvement and that is something to celebrate.

— c h a p t e r   s i x —

The Mental Healthcare "System"

It is important for you to know more about the children's mental health-care system. The system consists of the patients, their parents, guardians and advocates, the social workers, therapists, psychologists, psychiatrists, insurance companies, state and federal agencies and concerned community members. In a case where the child is suffering from a mild form a of mental illness, there are usually no problems with the system. The insurance company pays a large percentage of the child's medical bills, including medication. The parents usually make co-payments and everything seems to work out fine.

Things change when a child has a severe form of mental illness. All too often, the child needs more time with his professional than the insurance company will allow. The family is forced to turn to municipal or county government agencies or even state agencies for help, and usually requires a frustrating mountain of paperwork and an even more frustrating waiting period for the approval of services. This leaves parents wondering why the insurance companies don't give mental health problems the same financial level of care that they do physical problems and why politicians aren't doing something to make sure that mentally ill children get the care they need. Our government should force insurance companies to provide the same level of care that other physical illnesses are given. Parents and other advocates of the mentally ill often feel helpless and almost bullied by the system. Despite its problems, though, there are many positive aspects of the mental healthcare system.

The primary part of the system, which consists of dedicated mental healthcare professionals helping the mentally ill, often works quite well. These dedicated people work with parents, their mentally ill children, teachers, social workers, the juvenile justice system and other advocates to try and help the patients. This is the true heart of the mental healthcare system—the people who actually work together as a team to help mentally ill children. When people comment that the "system has no heart," they are sadly mistaken. The media rarely recognizes these stalwarts of the system, and instead only focuses on the seriousness of the problems within the outer perimeters of the mental healthcare system—the state and local governments who always seem to cut funding, the insurance companies who don't want to offer higher coverage and the occasional stories of a mentally ill person who harms or kills someone because the system failed him or her. While all of these stories certainly are important, they provide a one-sided view. Good things are happening at the core of the system every day. When more of the public becomes aware that the mentally ill and their families are human beings who need compassion and a helping hand, hopefully there will be more community support for the mentally ill and the services that help them.

When Mark and I first began advocating for Tommy, we knew nothing of how the mental healthcare system worked and we felt lost and confused. Mark and I felt as if we alone were struggling against Tommy's illness and that it was pulling the whole family down. One of the wisest things I have ever learned is that life can be filled with problems, but it's how you handle these problems that counts. You can't dwell on fears and anxieties, you have to conquer them.

Parents in situations like this often feel small and helpless against the system. When it comes to dealing with the government agencies in order to get help, the endless bureaucracy can be very intimidating. The government seems so big and powerful when it comes to this sort of confrontation. A parent is prone to feel as if he or she is alone against an entire group—a huge group for that matter. Is there anything that one person can do to change things? My answer is—plenty! Six years ago, we often faced what seemed like mountains when it came to dealing with the system, but we overcame these obstacles and obtained the help we needed for our son. You can do this for your child.

Have You Thanked Your Local Mental Healthcare Worker Today?
Recently, there has been a lot of publicity about problems in the mental healthcare system. While it is certainly important to make the public aware of these problems, these newspaper and magazine stories are not telling the whole story. Such articles are intended to increase public awareness and support, in the hopes that state government will increase funding to these programs and enact new laws to protect the mentally ill. I support that 100 percent. However, these articles have unintentionally made the whole system look seriously problematic. My experience with our local North Carolina county mental healthcare system has been excellent. I feel it is important to recognize what is right with the system, not focus only on what is wrong with it.

Tommy has a severe psychotic disorder, and is both violent and sexually reactive. "Sexually reactive" is a fancy term for a child that sexually molests others. Prior to our move to North Carolina, not one of the other states in which we lived had a program that would step in and help us with Tommy. Our insurance allowed for only thirty-five days of inpatient mental healthcare. Due to the severity of his problems, Tommy needed long-term residential care. Thank goodness we moved to North Carolina where my stepson has been certified "*Willie M.*" *Willie M.* is a program that insures that violent children get the mental healthcare and services needed to address their severe problems.

It took several weeks to get him certified, but it has been the best thing that ever happened to us. The process started with a referral to our local mental healthcare facility, Behavioral Healthcare, for help with the massive paperwork and documentation required to start the certification process. I must admit that I felt uneasy about dealing with a local mental health facility. We had been paying a small fortune already for Tommy's care and hadn't really gotten much help. I didn't expect any better from Behavioral Healthcare. Fortunately, I couldn't have been more wrong.

We found Behavioral Healthcare to be filled with dedicated professionals who really cared, not only for our mentally ill child, but for our family as well. My stepson was finally certified approximately six weeks after we first filled out the application. At that time, he had been hospitalized for those six weeks and our insurance had run out. Medicaid was now paying for the hospitalization, but Tommy needed residential care that Medicaid didn't cover fully. Things were really getting down to the wire. The people at Behavioral Healthcare offered not only help in expediting his application, but also offered support in this desperate time for our family. They even assigned us a case manager to help us have a contingency plan in place, should my stepson be released from the hospital due to loss of a pay source. Understanding the danger Tommy presented to our younger children, they assured us that they would help us find placement for him, in the interim, until *Willie M.* certification had a chance to come through. My stepson was so violent and sexually reactive that he was a danger to everyone in the family, especially the youngest children. Experience had taught us that short hospitalizations had only served to send him home angrier. Terrified that he might be sent home before he was stabilized—six weeks in the hospital had not yet stabilized him—we were praying for a miracle. *Willie M.* was approved for my stepson in mid-June, just in the nick of time.

Immediately after his certification, my stepson was assigned a wonderful case manager. We are so grateful to have her. She is one of the most concerned individuals that I have ever known. Tommy's case manager has spent countless hours working to see that my stepson gets the best care possible. Tommy is currently in a residential facility, in a treatment program for sexually reactive children. While he hasn't made a lot of progress, we know that all that can be done to help him is being done. Our case manager keeps us up to date on everything and we have developed trust in her. When parents have had bad experiences with the mental healthcare system, as many parents of mentally ill children have, they tend to trust no one. Our son's case manager has earned our trust by always telling us everything about our son's care. If we ask a question that she doesn't have an answer to, she finds out.

When you have a severely mentally ill child, especially one who acts out in a violent manner, all you ever seem to do is worry. You worry about getting your child the much-needed care they deserve. You worry about keeping your child's care once you get it. The worry tends to take precedence over just about everything else in your life. Having our case manager has assuaged our worries and given us back the chance to have lives again. Just last week, Tommy's hospital announced that it was closing. Under other circumstances, this would have been devastating news to us. Even before we got the news from the case manager, a plan was already in place to find him appropriate placement. Within two days, he was accepted into a new hospital with the necessary sexually reactive treatment program. We were fortunate enough to find out that the hospital was closing two days before it hit the newspapers. Can you imagine how upset we would have been reading it in the paper first?

Our trust in our son's case manager has kept us from worrying excessively. She visits our son regularly at the hospital and has met several times with his treatment team. My stepson was in a hospital three hours from our home. Visiting him required six hours of car travel, and our case manager made the trip at least once a month, just to make sure Tommy was getting proper care. We know she always has our son's, and even our family's, best interests, as her top priority. The new hospital is actually closer, only two hours away. It's supposed to be a good hospital, with a new sexually reactive treatment program for children under age twelve. Sometimes, things do work out for the best: Dedicated mental healthcare professionals can turn your whole family's life around.

Recent publicity has indicated that oftentimes the relationship between mental healthcare workers and the parents of the patient can turn adversarial. While it would be easy to lay the blame solely on the mental healthcare workers, I feel that sometimes it is also the responsibility of the parents. Living with a mentally ill child is a stress like no other. Frequently, parents are living in fear right in their own home. Children can be psychotic, sexually reactive and even homicidal. It's something most of us would prefer to think impossible, but I can assure you it's possible. I've had to live with it. Children like my stepson are particularly dangerous in the home. Every day is a struggle just trying to keep the other children safe. Day to day life is filled with nothing but fear and pain. This pain can often make parents overzealous when it comes to the way they deal with the very people who are trying to help them. Desperate to stop the stress and anxiety, parents can forget that a "team" approach will accomplish more than an adversarial one. Previous disappointments with the mental healthcare system can make parents suspicious of the people with whom they are dealing. In their passionate desire to help their sick child, parents often feel it best to come on like storm troopers when they ask for help. Sometimes, pain and desperation lead parents to feel they must fight the system even before there is a valid reason to do so. Instead of trying to view the system as a partnership, they view it as something from which they should demand help. Going into the situation pounding desks and demanding help that may not be immediately available just creates an atmosphere of tension, not cooperation. Everyone, parents included, ends up on the defensive. Often, a little patience and giving the mental healthcare workers the necessary time to work on resolving the problems will net good results. Cooperation benefits everyone; that's a proven fact.

Each local mental healthcare system is given a budget by higher powers. Having had the opportunity to get to know some of these professionals, I can assure other parents of the mentally ill that the people who work in these jobs are truly dedicated. They wouldn't be doing this job if they didn't have a strong desire to help others. Their jobs are obviously high-stress and dealing with the mentally ill can even be dangerous. Sometimes, they are even attacked by their clients. Having to work within a small, fixed budget causes frustration for them as much as it may for you. They occasionally have to deny care, based on financial decisions over which they have no control. Recently, there have even been accounts of healthcare workers misappropriating funds not for their own personal gain, but to help clients. The government, given the devotion showed in such acts, clearly should take note of the desperation for funds and provide these professionals with the funding their programs deserve.

Good mental healthcare workers have to be totally committed to helping the mentally ill. These people certainly aren't in it for the money. Most of them have master's degrees and get paid far less than they would in other professions. They still go to work every day, completely dedicated to their cause. The mental healthcare workers are just like everyone else that advocates for the mentally ill. They feel passionate about helping the mentally ill and are dedicated to doing so. It serves parents well to remember this. The system works best when everyone works as a team. Adversarial relationships just slow down the process.

Unnecessary lawsuits, often filed before trying to mediate the situation, make things worse for everyone. Sometimes frustrated parents and other advocates use lawsuits to go after the mental healthcare system when things don't go their way. Fighting these lawsuits takes more of the funding desperately needed to help the mentally ill. If everyone tries to remember that they are all on the same side, these situations could be resolved without such drastic measures. Stepping back and taking a look at the big picture could go a long way toward resolving the issues. Realizing that mental healthcare workers are trying to help us, not fight us, is something we all need to remember. These professionals get as frustrated as we do when they can't help. Taking our frustrations out on them isn't going to accomplish anything. It's always possible that with a little patience and a few well-written letters to state officials, you might find the help you need.

Parents and advocates for the mentally ill need to focus their energy on state and federal legislatures for more funding and laws to protect the mentally ill. I know firsthand that my county's state senator cares. His office even took the time to call me after I wrote to them explaining Tommy's situation. They gave me their assurance that they were looking into the problems I had experienced with the system. Writing a letter from the heart can sometimes be the best way to advocate for the mentally ill. Try it. You certainly have nothing to lose and everything to gain.

Something a lot of us take for granted is that our local mental healthcare workers are making our community safer, for all of us. At times, mentally ill people can be dangerous to both themselves and others. Some even commit unspeakably violent crimes. The mental healthcare system is set up to help treat these people, making our communities safer for everyone. They are even there to help when there is a crisis, providing help toward emergency hospitalization when needed. Personally, I am grateful that they are there to help. I know from my experience that they care about the safety of my family. Before my son got help, it was unsettlingly easy for our family to imagine that he could rape or kill someone when he got older and stronger. Now that he is getting help, we no longer see such a terrible possibility in his future. Thanks to the system, we feel more at ease that Tommy's future will not include violent crime, and the community can feel safer knowing that an infrastructure to safeguard them and their children functions as it is designed to.

Have you thanked your local mental healthcare worker today?

Anger Into Action

Anger and frustration are feelings that all parents of mentally ill children experience from time to time. Being the parent of a mentally ill child is very difficult and stressful. You feel angry that your child is sick and that your life has been turned upside down by your child's illness, and you feel frustrated that you can't seem to get the help he or she needs. These feelings are perfectly normal. But they must be dealt with if you ever hope to dispel them.

If allowed to fester, anger can do untold harm to the person who is experiencing it. Stress, a result of wallowing in angry and frustrated emotions, is thought to bring on many physical illnesses, including high blood pressure, strokes and heart attacks. Angry people can become bitter and withdrawn, even depressed. You have a mentally ill child, a spouse and maybe other children who love and need you. They need you to be healthy in order to be the best advocate and parent you can be. Stay healthy.

So, what do you do with all that anger? How do you handle situations that make you feel frustrated and incensed? The answer is to turn that fury into energy and transform that energy into positive action.

Here's how to change pent-up anger into what you need—**positive energy**.

1. Whenever you feel overwhelmed with angry feelings (or any neg-
    ative emotion), take a time-out and recognize what you are feeling.
    Releasing pent-up physical frustration in a positive way, such as
    exercise or even allowing yourself a good cry, will help to clear your
    mind. Once the physical manifestations of frustration have been
    released, you can then focus on the problem
2. Assess the situation. Review what has made you feel angry and
    begin thinking of positive ways in which you can take action to
    improve the situation. Spend time lying down in a quiet room, as
    relaxed as possible, when you do this. You can completely focus on
    the problem and possible solutions.
3. Formulate a plan of action. Often, formulating a tentative plan will
    begin to make you feel more in control and much better.
4. Take the first step! Something as simple as making a phone call to
    a professional agency or advocacy group who may be able to help
    your child can give you a sense of doing something positive to
    solve your problem.

Taking positive action toward solving a problem diffuses anger,
turning it into a useful positive force, your internal energy, which is
necessary to propel you toward finding a solution for your child's problem:

Understanding Your Anger + Positive Action = Positive Energy
Turning your anger and frustration into energy can give you just the
edge you need to effectively deal with the problems you face. One
example from my own personal experience conveys this:

Tommy had been admitted to a psychiatric hospital. After a month,
it was apparent that he needed long-term, residential treatment. We
had applied to get Tommy into a statewide program for violent children that would cover residential hospitalization, but this would take
about four weeks. We had only two weeks of hospitalization left that
would be covered by our insurance policy and then there would be a
two-week gap in coverage. Tommy had Medicaid to pick up the slack,

but because it had been determined that he needed residential care, we knew that Medicaid might pull its services at any minute, because they didn't fully cover residential care in our state. As the parents of eight children, we didn't have the ability to pay $1000.00 a day for his hospitalization. Things looked pretty scary.

Needless to say, I felt frustrated and very angry. I was angry that our insurance company didn't cover mental illness with the same level of coverage it gave physical illness. The hospital hadn't even been able to get Tommy stabilized yet and the insurance company was going to simply stop paying for his hospital care when his limit was up. It didn't matter than he hadn't been helped, just that he had a limited number of days in the hospital. I was angry that Medicaid didn't cover residential treatment. How could they not cover the sickest children's needs? I was angry that I felt so helpless and I was frustrated that I couldn't help Tommy myself. Needless to say, I was very much overwhelmed.

What did I do? Well, first I had a good, long cry, then I officially went into crisis mode. I focused on what I could do to help Tommy. I began to map out a plan of action. First, I would call one of my resources and find out whom I needed to call to ask for help. Then, I would call everyone that she suggested might be able to help me, explain my situation and make a heartfelt plea to these people. Having a plan is step one.

How to Handle Disappointing Setbacks

1. When a setback occurs, step back and take a critical look at the situation. Try to be calm and rational. This will help you to analyze the situation more effectively. By analyzing where things went wrong, you can learn from past mistakes and have more success the next time around.

2. Reformulate your original plan of action. Situations often change because they tend to evolve over time. Putting a new and improved plan into action will always make you feel better. The new plan will take away that feeling of helplessness and replace it with a feeling of being in better control of the situation.

3. Stay focused on the goal! Just keep moving forward, regardless of how many setbacks you experience. Just keep moving forward toward your goal. Don't give up just because the going

gets rough. Positive advocates have to keep going forward for the sake of the child they care about. Remember, there is always hope!

4. Celebrate each little success you experience on the way to getting help for your child. Advocating for a mentally ill child is hard work. Never forget to pat yourself on the back for a job well done!

chapter eight

Speaking from the Heart

As his or her advocate, you naturally feel passionate about helping your mentally ill child. Your love and empathy for that child are the forces that drive you to advocate for him or her. One of the most important things to remember when you speak to others about helping your child is that you must speak straight from the heart. Always remember to let those helping you know how much you appreciate their doing so. Even the people who can't or won't help you should be thanked for their time and consideration. Doing so will always keep the lines of communication open should you ever have reason to approach them again.

Sincere words that come from the heart of a loving parent or anyone else who loves someone enough to advocate for him or her are the most powerful words of all. Often, people in a position to advocate feel uncomfortable expressing their true feelings to those they must ask for help. If you feel this way, you must overcome this discomfort in order to be an effective advocate. Only when you open up about your feelings, can others truly understand and empathize with you.

I remember when we first started taking Tommy to doctors for help…it felt like my entire life was on display. Essentially, I felt naked in public. Telling his doctors and mental health professionals everything they needed to know in order to help him, made me feel like I didn't have one stitch of privacy left. There were times I wanted to clam up, but it didn't take long for me to realize that the only way to get Tommy any real help was for me to sacrifice the privacy of our family. These professionals needed to know about everything in Tommy's life in order to be able to understand and effectively diagnose him. Over time, I came to find that it was the only way.

When I began to understand their need to know about our life, I divulged more information. People were a lot more understanding and helpful than I ever thought they would be. Soon, I realized that by telling people what was in my heart, I was not only helping Tommy, but helping myself to feel better as well. I know firsthand that it's not easy to sacrifice your privacy, but you'll find the payoff for doing so is immeasurable.

Don't be afraid to let others know how you are feeling. Doing so allows others to empathize with you and your mentally ill child. You'd be surprised. Sometimes the passionate words from a loving parent's heart can open doors that might otherwise be closed if only negative methods were used. Understanding what you are going through can even make those with the power to help your child want to go the proverbial extra mile to help.

Being grateful for the help you might or do receive is a very powerful tool. Just because you have a child with a problem doesn't mean that others owe you help. This statement might make you feel angry, but allow me to explain further.

The mental healthcare system was formed because kind and compassionate people cared enough about the mentally ill to dedicate their lives to helping them. It wasn't formed just because people gave birth to children with problems. These gracious souls knew that the mentally ill really needed and deserved help. Of course, they were right, for every mentally ill individual deserves to be helped.

Most of the people who work in the mental healthcare system never hear the words "thank you." A lot of people think of the system as an inanimate object, instead of viewing it as a group of compassionate human beings who are there to help sick children and adults.

Make it a point to thank everyone who has or is trying to help your child. The first time we thanked some of these people, they were either surprised or outright shocked. Many said it was the first time that anyone had ever thanked them for doing their jobs.

That's a sad state of affairs. Recognize and appreciate those who try to help your child. This can only make their dedication to doing their jobs stronger. Speak from the heart. You are now well on your way to being your child's best hope for recovery, a positive advocate!

– c h a p t e r   n i n e –

Patience

Patience is a crucial virtue when it comes to dealing with the mental healthcare system. I know from experience that it's not always easy to be patient. However, I also know that being patient is definitely important when it comes to getting the right help for your child.

When you have a mentally ill child, especially one who is in critical condition, you want help for your child and you want it fast! This is a natural feeling and part of being a loving parent. All parents of mentally ill children know that they want their child to be well, or "fixed," if you will. Unfortunately, reality always steps in to smack us in the face. There are no quick fixes for mentally ill children. Yes, there can be amazing results with medications that seem to be quick fixes, but in most cases if the child goes off the medication the symptoms come back again.

As the parent of a mentally ill child, you must face the fact that a severe mental illness is a problem that only time and proper care will solve. Some medications can take weeks to become effective and therapy is a constant ongoing process toward healing. Unrealistic expectations concerning the length of time before your child will be better will only cause you unnecessary frustration. Instead, view it as a project in progress, but one that will have worthwhile results.

In some cases, it may even be necessary to face the fact that the problem may never get better. Tommy will need years, maybe even a lifetime, of medication and therapy, because he has such severe psychiatric problems. By facing the probability that his care will last a very long time, we have learned to deal with the situation more cooperatively. We have learned to accept the small steps he makes and to celebrate them. Taking things one day at a time keeps us from getting discouraged.

Whatever your child's prognosis, it doesn't mean that you have to give up hope. There is always hope! Research is being done every day in the area of mental illness. Research and new advances in treatment always offer hope, even in worst-case scenarios. Being a good advocate means that you are always on the lookout for new ways to help your child. A true advocate might get discouraged sometimes, but absolutely never gives up! Just take a step back, assess the situation and look for new ways of dealing with the problem.

You cannot expect a doctor or therapist to just come in, talk briefly to your child, give the child a pill and problem solved. Mentally ill children cannot be "fixed" by a magic pill. They are helped by weeks, months and sometimes even years of therapy, doctor's appointments, hospital visits and, when needed, medication. Each case is different. Some will respond quickly; some will take longer. There is no real way to accurately predict this. Your child's mental health professional can only give you an estimate of treatment time. Please don't expect him or her to give you more than that. Mental illness is often unpredictable. Changes, such as weight loss or gain, environmental changes or even puberty in your child can necessitate changes in medication or therapy. To be a positive advocate you must develop the patience to allow the mental healthcare professional to have all the time he or she needs to treat your child. When your child is in treatment, take it day by day instead of focusing solely on the big picture. Then you will develop the patience necessary to deal with this often unpredictable situation.

The first step to developing patience is to realize that the problem didn't crop up overnight and it can't be fixed overnight. I have heard this from many different professionals. Treating mental illness is complicated, especially when it comes to children. Children often lack the skills to effectively communicate what is wrong. Doctors and mental health professionals must piece together a complete picture of the child through parents, schools, medical records, etcetera, and this can take time. A truly competent professional takes time before making a diagnosis. This may be frustrating for everyone involved. In most cases, though, it should not take more than several visits. You want the best care your child can get. Rushing the professional won't help your child and it may even damage your ability to communicate with the person. Do everything you can to provide the mental healthcare professional with the information needed. That will keep you busy and help the professional at the same time. Do be aware, though, that occasionally a professional may take an inordinate amount of time to diagnose your child. Such indecision may indicate confusion, inexperience or that they are outside of their area of expertise.

Some of the hardest news that you may have to face as the parent of a mentally ill child, is the fact that your child may have a discouraging prognosis. Tommy, for instance, has several psychiatric problems that complicate his treatment. Realistically, his prognosis indicates that his problems probably will last a lifetime. I say probably, because the fact is that no one really knows for sure. Tearfully, my husband and I were forced to face this prognosis when he was about six years old. It took us a while to be able to accept this, but given time, we realized that we had to face the facts. Denying the reality of the situation only prolongs the inevitable. You ultimately will have to accept that your child has a mental illness that may take years of treatment to correct or stabilize, maybe even a lifetime. Denial doesn't help anyone; it merely stalls you from taking action that might really contribute to helping your child.

We take things one small step at a time. This works for us, making life so much less stressful when we focus on the present and not what the future may hold for Tommy. Sure, sometimes we still have days when we cry, but we just pick ourselves back up and start concentrating on the small steps again. Each small step can bring you great joy, if you let it. Find the best professionals to treat your child. Then trust the people to be dedicated and empathetic. Concentrate on doing what you can to help them and on what you can do to help your child, not on how long it will take. You must just be patient and let those trying to help your child do their jobs.

A Note from Dr. Pastore: *"I am struck by the possibility that being a good advocate ultimately also includes being patient with yourself, accepting your own limits as a parent, and surrendering some of the normal controls we, as parents, strive so hard to maintain with regard to raising our children while finding new ways of maintaining a safe and nurturing environment."*

— c h a p t e r   t e n —

How Can You Help?

Ask for periodic parent/therapist conferences, without the child present! Decisions regarding treatment options and duration of treatment only should be discussed between the parent/advocate and the mental healthcare professional. Should a discussion in which your child is present begin to turn toward subjects that shouldn't be spoken of in front of him or her, either have the child return to the waiting room or continue the conversation at another time. The child should hear an age-appropriate version of the conversation, with a chance for them to give their own input if they are capable.

What if things don't continue to progress? What if they get worse? One of the most valuable things I have learned about children with serious mental illness is that the illness will often fluctuate. Realizing this greatly reduced my stress level when Tommy would relapse: I kept in mind that it was part of a cycle. Some children continue to make steady progress, eventually even recovering from their illness. It really just depends on the nature and severity of the mental illness.

A qualified mental healthcare professional will want to develop a crisis plan for your child before a crisis arrives. While this may seem like an uncomfortable and unnecessary topic of discussion, he or she will need your presence and input, along with that of other members of the treatment team, to effectively put the plan into place. If your child's mental healthcare professionals recommend a crisis plan, trust their judgment. Don't let the idea of a crisis plan frighten you, as many times, such a plan never has to be put into motion. If your child does experience a mental health crisis, trust me, you will be glad that the plan had already been formulated. Crisis plans help you to remain calm during a period of upheaval, because you have written instructions as to what to do in case of a crisis. Preparing such a plan in advance of a mental health emergency just makes good sense!

What are some of the best courses of action to take during a crisis period? The first thing I always recommend is to start by making phone calls. Start by consulting your child's psychiatrist and other designated mental healthcare professionals. They are the best people to recommend how to handle a crisis situation and whether hospitalization may or may not be necessary. Don't be afraid to ask what other options may be available, if hospitalization is recommended. You have a right to make an informed decision regarding your child.

When Tommy needed more than just the help of a regular psychiatrist, I began doing research on the hospitals that were available to him for treatment. By asking people at the local mental healthcare center about resources for this information, I was able to contact people who directed me to a program that was just right for Tommy's needs. When the time for actual hospitalization arrived, I was prepared for it. We knew who the best doctor to treat him was and just where to send him to get this treatment. My phone calls for information allowed me to feel more in control of a very out-of-control situation.

There is something very important to remember when you are making these kinds of phone calls. The people you are talking to chose to be in the mental healthcare profession, because they want to help the mentally ill. It's okay to call and ask for help. It's even okay to cry. This is the time to go straight from the heart. Tell these people your situation and how you feel. If the crisis is serious, if it puts your family in immediate danger of harm from the mentally ill child or if the child might harm him- or herself, convey this point emphatically. That's why they call it a crisis: Something needs to be done and done quickly. Always remember to thank the person to whom you are talking, even if the person is unable to help you. Remember, this keeps the door open for future reference. If the person is unable to help, ask them who you might call instead. Often, just asking this will open up several new resources to you. Call the new resources they have given you. Keep trying until you find the answers you are looking for.

Sometimes being an advocate means that you have to temporarily pour all of your energy into helping that child. I stress the word temporarily here. You must also realize that the other children in the family need you, too. Set aside certain hours of the day to make your calls, for example, utilizing the down time available during school hours or naptime.

It is said that the pen is mightier than the sword. In my case, it was my home computer. My computer gave me the power of the written word and access to the immeasurable volume of information on the Internet. Whether composed by hand or computer, the written word can be your most useful tool in getting help and services for your child from any number of sources.

While there is certainly no guarantee that positive advocacy will always bring the results you want, I truly believe it to be the most effective approach to getting help for your mentally ill child. I have personally seen positive advocacy open doors that most likely would have been closed if I'd tried to use strong-arm methods. The valuable lesson that I learned from writing just one letter to a senator was that asking for help in an appreciative way and not demanding it seems to yield positive results.

The ability to sway feelings, gain help and positively advocate using the written word is easily demonstrable: For example, I was devastated for Tommy when the state legislature took away the *Willie M.* program some time after he had been admitted to the program. It was heartbreaking for parents of children like Tommy to see such a secure program simply voted into oblivion. I felt the best and most positive way to react was to accept the decision—what other choice was there?—and try and support the new programs the state planned to put in place. I did come upon a rather unique opportunity to tell the state how I felt about losing the program. I was asked to write an article for a magazine that is read by many of the state legislators. The purpose of the article was to talk about the people local mental heath facilities were serving—in particular, Tommy.

Given this forum, I wanted to say two things. First, I wanted to tell the state what a good job our local mental healthcare facility was doing to help my stepson. I felt that the mental healthcare facility in our county was excellent and deserved recognition. I hoped that the state would take the hint and model other community mental health facilities after the one in our county.

Second, I wanted to make the state aware of what was lost when they cancelled the *Willie M.* program. I didn't use the article to blast them for taking it away. I used my positive methods and merely wrote my deepest feelings from the bottom of a mother's heart. Far better to touch the heart than to alienate the intended audience. I heard the article touched a lot of people. For that, I am grateful. Maybe somewhere along the line, someone will strive to make the new program even better than the *Willie M.* was. I'm keeping my fingers crossed. I have high hopes for the future.

Remember, as I've mentioned before, to take care of yourself during these times of crisis with your mentally ill child. When I first started advocating for Tommy, I often forgot to take time for myself. My enthusiasm for helping him quickly allowed his problems to become the total focus of my life. It didn't take too long for me to end up exhausted and out-of-touch with my own needs. While concentrating on helping a child is crucial, don't forget that there are other aspects of living that are very important. If you are married, don't forget that your spouse needs time with you, too. Keeping the marriage intact is very important to the well-being of your children. Take time to just go and do something fun and reaffirm your relationship. If you have other children, don't forget that they need time with their mom and dad. Mental illness in children can be so overwhelming that it affects the whole family.

It is also important to remember that there is more to life than mental illness. Dealing with a mentally ill child can be so overwhelming that it can completely take over your life. Don't let it! To be an effective advocate, you need to stay in the best possible emotional shape. Taking care of your own needs helps you to do that. One of the most important things you can do to help your mentally ill child is to take good care of yourself. They need you to be at your best at all times. Taking extra good care of yourself will help you be just that and give you the emotional and physical strength you need to positively advocate for your mentally ill child.

Things You Can Do When Your Child Is In Crisis
1. ENACT YOUR CRISIS PLAN!
2. Call your child's mental healthcare providers for advice!
3. Ask your child's professionals what the treatment options are.
4. Consider your available options and make a decision regarding them.
5. Take action regarding your child's mental healthcare professionals' recommendations.
6. Make phone calls to get information and reassurance regarding treatment options.
7. If your child is a danger to himself or others, he or she may need hospitalization.
8. Hospitalize the child if needed.
9. *Call 911 immediately* if your mentally ill child is currently posing a physical threat to you or anyone else. The police are equipped to handle a dangerous situation.
10. Remember to take care of yourself in times of crisis

It is important to note that you will need a crisis plan if your mentally ill child is acting out and becoming enraged. This plan should be formulated in advance or in anticipation, of a violent episode. While definitely not pleasant to think about, a sound plan is crucial to the safety of both the mentally ill child and the family. This plan can best be formulated with the help of your child's mental health professionals.

In some cases, it may be necessary to learn to restrain a violent child. While the mere idea of restraining a child seems upsetting, it may sometimes be necessary to protect the child from hurting himself or others. The professionals working with your child are the best ones to instruct you on methods of restraint, if they recommend it.

Crisis plans are composed of the steps you should take in an immediate crisis situation, in which the mentally ill person is violent. It usually has numbers to call in a crisis clearly posted on it. If the crisis situation is truly dangerous, call 911 first. Policemen are better trained to handle dangerous individuals. Keeping yourself and your family members safe must always be your top priority. Consult your child's mental healthcare professionals to find out if you need a crisis plan for your child.

Note from Dr. Pastore: *"Your other children should know the parts of the crisis plan that effects them. Ask them a pertinent question that could help them in a critical or dangerous situation, for example: What should you do when your brother or sister starts hitting himself, a sibling, a parent, or other person?"*

– c h a p t e r   e l e v e n –

The Other Children in the Family

Having a mentally ill child in your family won't affect only the child who is sick and his or her parents/advocates. The other children in the family will be affected, too. Sometimes they will feel jealous of the attention that their mentally ill sibling is getting or frustrated that their parents are so preoccupied with their brother or sister. These feelings are all perfectly normal and they do deserve to be addressed. Talk to your other children about their feelings—often! Maintaining a sense of open communication with your other children will help you keep on top of what they are feeling and help you to address these feelings sooner.

One thing that I found during our ordeal was that my children matured very quickly and because of that, Mark and I tried to give them detailed explanations of Tommy's illness and treatment. We learned about mental illness as a family. Mark and I talked to them openly and answered their questions honestly. Since they observed their brother's illness firsthand, we thought it to be in their best interests to educate them. In the end, teaching them about mental illness seemed to help them be more patient and understanding with Tommy.

My experience as a mother has taught me that our honest and open approach was a fruitful one. If children see their parents upset or crying, they may take those feelings personally and blame themselves, even when they have done nothing wrong. By explaining to them the reason that you are upset, they will understand the situation that much better. This also provides great opportunity to talk to your children about the fact that some things in life are quite serious. Children tend to learn through example. If they see you advocating positively and turning your frustration into a positive force, then there is a good chance they will do the same when they confront problems of their own

Explaining mental illness to older children is difficult though possible, but explaining mental illness to a very young child presents a challenge. When my youngest son Jake, then age four, asked what was wrong with Tommy and why he was in the hospital, I told him, "Because he did bad things." When he asked, if he did bad things would he go to the hospital too, I was shocked that he would even think such a thing. I realized that in his mind he had come to the conclusion that children who acted badly were sent away to the hospital. I suddenly remembered that Mark and I had packed all of Tommy's clothes, put him in the van and driven him to the hospital. It hit me that what I thought had made no impression on him had made a huge one instead. It seemed at the time that he was too little to understand what was going on.

So, how do you explain mental illness to a small child? There's obviously no definitive answer, but I developed a child-friendly approach that I used to explain Tommy's mental illness to Jake. I am proud to say that several therapists have since asked if they could use my method to explain mental illness to their young patients.

"What's the matter with Tommy?"

The day my youngest son Jacob asked me about Tommy, I was lying on my bed, reading some papers the hospital had sent me. Jake curled himself up beside me and asked, "Mommy, will you always love me?"

"Of course I will, Jake. Why do you ask?"

"Do you love Tommy?"

"Yes, I do."

"Even when he was being bad?" Jake asked, his eyes looking straight into mine.

"Yes, Jake, even when he was being bad."

"Then why did Daddy take him away to live in the hospital? Is that where you take kids when they are bad?" Jake looked at me, anxious for an answer. "If I'm bad, will Daddy take me to the hospital, too?"

Tears were beginning to well up in my eyes. Obviously, Jake thought that Mark had taken Tommy to the hospital simply because he was behaving badly. Unfortunately, Jake had witnessed some terrible things. Even at the young age of four, he knew that what Tommy had done was wrong. It had never occurred to me that what he had seen Tommy doing had made such an impression on him or that I would have to talk to him about mental illness. I realized with a shock that he thought the psychiatric hospital was punishment for misbehavior and he was worried that if he misbehaved, he would be taken to the mental hospital as well. I realized that I should have explained earlier the difference between the nature of Tommy's mental illness and regular childhood misbehavior. But I let that thought go and entertained the new one that said the time had come to clear things up for Jake.

Taking Jake into my arms, I tried to hold back the tears as I searched for a way to explain mental illness to him. Carefully I navigated around things that would scare him or worry him further and then it hit me. I stumbled upon a way to tell him about mental illness that would give him a clear picture of what was wrong with his stepbrother.

"Jake," I said, "let's talk about the brain. It's inside your head and it's what makes you do the things that you do. Everyone has a brain. Mommy has one. Daddy has one. Bobby has one. Sissy has one. Tommy has one and you have one. Do you understand so far?"

"Yes, Mommy."

"Well, a healthy brain has a different color then one that is sick. Let's say that a healthy brain is the color blue. What are some things that are blue?"

"The sky," he answered, "and the walls."

"Very good, Jake. Mommy, Daddy, Bobby, Sissy and you all have healthy blue brains. Our brains work very well and help us to behave nicely."

"What about Tommy's brain?" Jake questioned, looking eerily

inquisitive for a four-year-old.

"Well, Tommy's brain isn't blue like yours and mine. His brain is very sick. It is the color red. Tell me what things might be the color red?"

"Apples," said Jake, "and my pants."

"That's right," I told him, "very good. They are all red, just like Tommy's brain."

"But why is Tommy's brain red, not blue like Bobby's and mine?"

"Well, when Tommy was a little boy, something happened inside his head that made his brain turn red. That's what we call mental illness. But don't worry, your brain is just fine because it is blue."

"Yeah, and not red like Tommy's. Will Tommy's brain ever turn blue again?" Jake looked up at me sadly.

"We don't know for sure, but we hope that someday it will turn blue again. That's why he's at the hospital. They are giving him medicines and therapy and trying to make his brain turn blue again."

"I hope it does!" Jake seemed to understand that his stepbrother was getting help at the hospital, not being punished. He smiled and said, "I love you, Mommy." He kissed my face and leapt off the bed. He ran straight up front where I heard him loudly exclaim, "Hey, Bobby, you know what? Your brain is blue just like mine!"

"Wow!" Bobby said in his usual excited manner. "A blue brain!" Bobby always took things very literally and seemed to accept the fact that his brother had a blue brain. Both boys then resumed whatever game they were playing while I breathed a sigh of relief. Thankfully, I had found a way to explain mental illness to him, but I chided myself for not having talked to him about mental illness sooner.

Though Jake didn't really understand what mental illness was as an older child would, he was able to relate to the concept that because his brain was a different color than that of his stepbrother, he was not mentally ill. As Jake grows older, I will be able to build upon this foundation and explain Tommy's illness to him in more concrete terms. For now though, this red and blue brain comparison was enough to ease his worries.

If you have a mentally ill child in the hospital, please take the time to talk to all of your other children, whatever their age, about the true meaning of the situation. You have the power to reassure them and clear up any misconceptions that they may have about mental illness. While you are at it, hug, kiss and tell them you love them a lot. Not just during a crisis period, but always. Showing love and affection is a very powerful and positive way to help your children grow.

– c h a p t e r   t w e l v e –

Talking to Family and Friends About Your Child's Mental Illness

When family members or friends ask about your mentally ill child, use the opportunity to educate them about your child's illness, medication and treatment. Don't be afraid to tell them exactly what is wrong. Not telling them about the problem may make your child seem scary to them. This may cause family members or friends to isolate themselves from the child, thinking they need to do so for their own protection. This is the last thing that you or your mentally ill child will find beneficial. The more you explain the condition thoroughly and treat it as you would any other illness, the more others will be able to accept it. We don't shy away from people who have serious physical illnesses. The mentally ill need the same kind of support.

Often, you may get advice from your parents or friends about "what to do" with your child. Sometimes, they may make rather cold and hurtful sounding suggestions like, "You really need to put him away. He is destroying your life." While the advice, as in the case of a violent child like Tommy, may carry some truth, the decision as to how to treat the child should not be influenced by the opinions of non-professionals. As a parent or advocate, you must always follow your child's professional's advice, your own gut instincts and your heart when it comes to making treatment decisions for your child.

Now, what does this mean in regards to your relationships with family and friends who offer advice? The first thing to remember is that most people give you this advice because they care about you and your mentally ill child. While it is easy to get angry when someone offers you unwanted advice about your child, try not to let your emotions ruin your relationship with the person. Unwelcome comments can actually open the doors of communication a little wider, giving you a chance to educate the individual about mental illness.

Your own openness about the subject of mental illness will eventually influence those around you. By finding that you are open, honest and not embarrassed to talk about your child's mental illness, others will be relieved. It may take a while, so just keep talking. Eventually, family members and friends will see that you are comfortable with the subject matter and will begin to allow themselves to feel comfortable with it, too. Old taboos are hard to erase, but mental illness is becoming less stigmatized every day.

— c h a p t e r   t h i r t e e n —

Asking for Help from Others

Most people do not like to ask for help for many reasons—embarrassment, shyness or fear of not getting what they ask for to name a few. If you are going to advocate for a mentally ill child, you will have to overcome shyness, forget about embarrassment and take a chance on requesting help from others in positions to help your child, but who are not mental health professionals.

Next we will talk about getting help beyond that of a mental healthcare professional. If your child is severely mentally ill, you will more than likely have to approach the school system, state and government agencies at some point in your advocacy to find additional help for your child. Do not be afraid.

I want to share with you what I consider the most powerful advocacy instrument of all—a heartfelt letter. A letter is tangible. People can hold it in their hand and read it, read it again and even pass it on for someone else to read. When it comes to asking for help from an agency, either municipal, state or federal, I always like to start with a letter that comes straight from my heart. If you speak from the deepest depths within you, it tends to reach the reader. Don't be afraid to express yourself; you just might be surprised at the response you get.

I have received wonderful responses from my state senator, several congressmen, the speaker of the house and even the governor. My letters were able to reach them, to touch them in ways that a phone call probably never could have. Phone calls are great if time is an issue and are also perfectly acceptable when you have gotten to know the person you are asking for help. But when it comes to initial contact, I truly recommend a personal letter.

There is one very important thing you need to remember when you write to someone asking for help. They did not make your child mentally ill. Many advocates, especially those new to advocacy and under tremendous stress, write angry letters to people from whom they want help. With such a letter, you could close a door that you may need open later. Always try to remember to be nice to everyone, whether they can help you at that moment or not.

A letter detailing exactly what the problem is, asking politely for help and thanking them for any assistance they could possibly provide is the one to which you will get the best reception. Appeal to the recipient's sense of humanity.

Writing Positive Advocacy Letters

The written word is often the very best way to communicate with those you are asking to help your mentally ill child for several reasons. It allows you to carefully compose your thoughts and present them in a manner that can be easily reviewed.

Verbal communication has never been my personal strong point. I tend to get nervous when speaking to people. This is not to say that I won't speak to people. In a crisis situation, I have been known to spend hours talking to people, soliciting their help for my stepson. By turning my anger into energy, I actually did quite well in communicating verbally. I do, however, strongly prefer written communication.

Letters written straight from the heart of a parent can do wonders when asking for help for a mentally ill child. Moreover, letters are tangible objects that cannot be deleted or ignored. If the reader is not able to help you, he can easily pass a letter on to someone who can. This has been the case several times in my advocacy experience.

Important Things To Remember When Writing an Advocacy Letter

- Write straight from the heart. Don't be afraid to let your feelings show in your letter. If your child is in crisis, convey that point emphatically. People can't empathize with you, unless they know what it is that you are experiencing.

- Always remember to tell the people to whom you are writing that you appreciate the jobs they do and you are grateful that they took the time to read your letters.

- State your problem clearly. It is important to focus on conveying just what the actual problem is. List any possible positive solutions to the problem.

- If you are asking for help, do so with gratitude. Remember, those who help the mentally ill do so because they care. Being thanked for helping is something they don't often hear. They will appreciate that you recognize they are doing important jobs to help the mentally ill.

- Always include your personal information: name, address, phone number, work number, fax, or e-mail address. They cannot respond to your letters unless they know how to contact you.

- Write letters to the supervisors of the people who help your mentally ill child and you on a regular basis. This boosts their morale by letting them know you appreciate the job that they do to help you. Writing a positive letter will also make you feel good and remind you just how lucky you are to have those people helping your mentally ill child.

- Don't be afraid to take a long shot. Go ahead; write to your local, state or federal official. You can even write to the President of the United States if you think it will help your child. Your voice deserves to be heard.

Mentally ill children often present a special challenge to their schools and teachers. As their children's advocates, parents usually have to inform the school of their child's problems and establish the introduction of the educators into the team that is striving to help their child. Educators can provide important insight into the child, as teachers spend roughly seven hours a day with him or her. Teachers may be aware of behavioral problems that the parents are not. Having your child's teachers as part of the team is often very valuable.

The most important thing to remember about teachers and school administrators is that they are not mental healthcare professionals and advocating with them will be very different from advocating in the mental health system. Due to the recent rash of school shootings, mental illness in children is now at the forefront of the news. While this is horribly tragic for those who have suffered because of shootings, this newfound awareness of mental illness in youngsters can produce more understanding on the part of teachers and administrators. We all now are realizing prevention is much preferable to dealing with the aftermath of violence.Teachers and school administrators now are learning everything they can about how to spot troubled children and how to help them.

As the mother of a child with a serious mental illness for whom violent behavior was an offshoot, it offers me relief to see school systems becoming more aware of these kinds of problems. I had the moral obligation to tell the school about Tommy's anger problems so that others would be protected from him. Because of the limited knowledge his teachers had of mental illness, they found it hard to accept that a six-year-old could have homicidal instincts.

While teachers are becoming better educated on the subject of mentally ill and disturbed children, you must be aware that they probably will not have the same understanding of a child's specific condition that a mental healthcare provider will. It may be necessary to give additional information to your child's school regarding the specifics of his or her illness. This can be accomplished through meetings, providing the school administration with written materials that detail the problem or even by giving the school permission to talk to your child's mental healthcare provider. Remember, everyone needs to work together as a team for the benefit of the child. Though you may think that giving this sort of information is an invasion of your family's privacy, you must keep in mind that to completely understand your child, the school must know as much as possible about him or her.

A good first step is to organize a meeting for all of your child's teachers and administrators so that you can discuss the problem together at the same time. Schools were always rather surprised that my husband and I were so open about Tommy's problems and not in utter denial, like many parents they dealt with. If you are called to the school for a meeting with teachers and administrators, know that most of them expect parents to be defensive, maybe even angry, when they say that there is a problem with their child. Don't let something like a label of "mentally disabled" upset you. It's simply a designation intended to help get necessary services, not to insult your child. It is important to note that you should do everything you can to make sure your child is labeled appropriately. If you feel that your child's problems are more serious than the school perceives them to be, you can request that your child be evaluated to insure that he or she gets the correct label and therefore appropriate services. If an evaluation is undertaken, make sure that you provide the school personnel with all the information they request, as well as any additional information that could help them determine your child's correct placement. This presents an excellent opportunity to include your child's mental health professional in the educational placement process.

Most teachers, just like mental healthcare workers, are dedicated to their profession. Both groups do what they do, because they genuinely care about other human beings. Always try to remember that when dealing with educators. Treat them with the kindness and respect with which you would like to be treated. This will reinforce the teamwork that is so necessary to getting your child the services he or she needs.

Example of a Positive Advocacy Letter

Name
Address
Phone Number
Fax Number

Date

Dear Salutation,

I am the mother of a child who suffers from severe mental illness. Our child has been hospitalized at [name of hospital] for the last three weeks. Our insurance company has informed us that his limited number of covered mental hospitalization days is about to expire. Because insurance companies are not legally obligated to cover mental healthcare with the same level of coverage as physical healthcare, my child will soon be released from [name of hospital].

His doctors have worked hard to try and stabilize my son, but have had no success so far. My child essentially will be returned to the home in the same mental state as before he was hospitalized. Because my child suffers from a psychotic disorder, he can easily become violent and is a danger to my family. We have applied for state aid to cover an extended stay in the hospital, but must wait several weeks to receive it. Past experience has taught us that short hospitalizations only send him home angrier than before he left. The ideal solution would be to have him remain hospitalized until he can at least be stabilized, while waiting for the state aid to begin covering his hospitalization expenses. Our state could certainly benefit from a program that helps families pay mental healthcare expenses, while waiting for state aid to begin, and whose insurance has been depleted. This would provide tremendous relief to worried parents such as myself.

I am writing to you, because you are the head of the state's health-care reform committee. Having heard you speak on the local news programs regarding these issues many times, I can tell that you are a man who cares deeply for the mentally ill children in our state. My spouse and I would be extremely grateful for any assistance you might be able to render regarding our situation. If you are unable to help us with this pressing problem, could you please provide me with the information that I need to contact someone else who can possibly help my child continue to receive the inpatient care he so desperately needs? Thank you for taking the time to read my letter and for any help you can provide.

Sincerely,

Signature

chapter fourteen

Reasonable Requests
and a Word About Lawsuits

No method of advocacy guarantees that you will get what you are asking for all of the time. That is simply unrealistic. You can, however, choose to view the denial of requests you make as a learning experience and use that experience to your advantage.

First, ask yourself why the request was denied. If you don't know the answer, try to find out. It is not unreasonable to call the people that denied the services or aid for your child and politely ask why your request was turned down. However, do refrain from yelling at them or being rude. The respectful, kind and grateful approach indicative of positive advocacy is best and, in some cases, could bring about reconsideration.

Second, reevaluate your request. Is it reasonable? If your request is being denied repeatedly, it may be that what you're requesting is not doable. For example: Let's say you have a child who is violent and in need of urgent care and is receiving services from the state through the local mental healthcare center. A reasonable request would be for this child to be hospitalized, so that he could get treatment and others would be safe from him. An unreasonable request would be for the mental healthcare system to provide a twenty-four hour-a-day aide/bodyguard for your child. This an unreasonable request for two reasons. The first is the cost of such twenty-four hour, seven day a week care. The second and most important reason is that if a child is so dangerous and sick that he needs someone to watch him twenty-four hours a day, then that child clearly needs hospitalization. At the hospital there is a whole staff available to watch him for the entire day and night to make sure he will not injure others or himself. No round-the-clock aide can possibly do the job of an entire hospital staff. Always make sure that what you are asking for is a reasonable request.

A Word About Lawsuits

As the parent of a mentally ill child, you can file a lawsuit against mental healthcare systems to get help for your child if you feel the child is not getting the aid he or she needs. This particular cross road is something that needs to be considered very seriously before you take action. Lawsuits should only be used as a last resort when all other methods of advocacy have failed. And if you choose to take such action, serious thinking needs to be done beforehand.

Considerations Before You File a Lawsuit:

1. Have all other avenues of solving the problem been exhausted?
2. Is there any other way I can find appropriate help for my child?
3. Am I filing this lawsuit because I am angry and frustrated or is there real merit to the case?
4. What are the possible personal consequences of my filing this lawsuit?
   a. Loss of time at work and reduced wages
   b. Loss of family time
   c. Added stress to myself and my family
   d. Legal fees
5. Will winning this case open new doors for my child and others?

As you can see, there is much more to consider when filing a lawsuit than just the fact that you might win or lose, as the case may be. Consider the possible consequences of legal action carefully when making a decision to sue. Valuable time and resources are used up when local mental health systems are sued. This could be detrimental not only to your child but to other deserving children as well. Local mental health systems have fixed budgets and lawsuits cause serious depletion of their funds and subsequent denial of services to others, maybe even your own child. Think very carefully and give yourself time to calm down if you're angry or frustrated before acting. You may realize that there are other more positive ways to handle your child's problem.

Each parent must follow his or her own conscience when it comes to filing lawsuits. There have been a couple of times where I had grounds to sue on Tommy's behalf, but, after careful consideration, Mark and I determined that the price our family would have paid in stress was not worth it to us. Thinking the situation through, we were able to find more positive and effective ways of dealing with the situation.

Perhaps it is the buildup of frustration over denied requests for quality care that causes lawsuits to be filed. Considering what parents of mentally ill children have to go through to get their voices heard and the many failures they must endure, it is not surprising. But failure is a part of the challenge you must accept when advocating for a mentally ill child.

– c h a p t e r   f i f t e e n –

Stay Focused

The two most important words of advice I can say to any advocate are, "Stay focused!"

These two words are very powerful and have kept me going through the darkest situations. When it looked like finding help for Tommy was hopeless, I often called my mother in California to get some much needed support. In each tearful conversation she would tell me, "Just stay focused on your goal, Beth, just stay focused!"

One afternoon after talking with my mom, I began to think about what those two little words meant. I came to realize that of course there would be setbacks trying to handle Tommy's illness, but the point was that I needed to focus on my goal of getting long-term help for Tommy and not let setbacks throw me for a loop. When I experienced a pitfall, I needed to step back, reevaluate the situation and refocus my attention on the big picture. By taking the focus off the negatives and directing my energies towards the ultimate goal, I could remain constantly motivated.

Those two words set me free! No longer was I wallowing in self-pity when I came upon a setback. When I did I repeated those words to myself and began to think about why I had experienced the setback and what my plan was to keep moving forward. The words "stay focused" took away my stress and replaced it with stronger motivation to keep heading toward the help that I knew was out there for my stepson. Ultimately, staying focused allowed me to succeed in finding Tommy the help he so desperately needed.

The great thing about the mindset of staying focused is that it quickly permeates other areas of your life. You begin to notice that life's little problems don't cause you as much stress. Instead, lessons from the setbacks are quickly processed and used constructively by your mind to plan your continued move forward. So much of the stress we experience in life is caused when we allow ourselves to get bogged down by life's abundance of problems and frustrations. Learning from things that go wrong, formulating a new plan and quickly moving forward relieves that stress greatly. Life is really just a learning experience. I have learned to see the joy in overcoming the obstacles that I have had to face, and maintaining a strong focus on my goals has allowed me to do so.

Four Steps to Help You Stay Focused:

Step back! When a setback occurs, step back and take a look at the situation from a non-emotional standpoint. This will help you to analyze the situation more critically. Analyze where and when things go wrong, learn from your mistakes and, hopefully, you will have more success the next time around.

Reformulate your original plan! Situations change because they tend to evolve over time. Make corrections. Put the new and improved plan into action.

Keep your attention on the goal! Keep moving forward, regardless of how many setbacks you have. Don't give up because the going gets rough. Being a positive advocate means you just keep going ahead toward that goal of finding help for your child, no matter how many times you face setbacks. Focus on the future: There is always hope!

Celebrate! Each little success you experience on the way to your goal of helping your mentally ill child deserves celebration. Advocating is hard work. Never forget to pat yourself on the back for a job well done.

Staying focused is easy to do and is a great form of personal empowerment. It puts your energy right where it needs to be, into getting help for your child. When problems occur, just tell yourself, "Stay focused!" over and over until it becomes second nature. Use the four steps to maintain focus. It will definitely take time, but your work will be well worth the effort if you finally achieve your goal of getting the best help for your mentally ill child.

chapter sixteen

Support Groups
and Positive Advocacy

Sharing feelings with other parents who are experiencing the same things that you are is often beneficial. There are also advocacy organizations that strive to bring parents together to advocate for the mentally ill. I would, however, like to interject a word of caution regarding these groups.

Support groups should make you feel better, not worse. If the focus of the group is primarily on anger over the mental healthcare system, you probably will only end up more stressed than before you joined. Remember, anger is a powerful emotion that, when properly focused, can be a tremendous energy force when used to advocate positively. Many groups mean well, but sometimes fall into the rut of dwelling on angry or hurt feelings, instead of trying to figure out how to take positive action to alleviate their feelings of misery.

Joining a support group could be very helpful, especially to someone who is just beginning to experience what it is like to have a mentally ill child. If the group you join makes you feel better and you feel that you get valid advice from its members, by all means continue.

Positive advocacy is a relatively new concept when it comes to getting help for the mentally ill. It has worked remarkably well for me in getting aid for my stepson and for many other people who have tried it. It reduces your stress and teaches you to view setbacks as challenges, not as failures. I know it can work for anybody who actively tries. If you already have a support group and their focus is negative, try setting a positive example when it comes to advocacy. As my husband says, "Positive advocacy is infectious—in a nice way." Advocate positively and you may have the satisfying experience of watching your positive example spread throughout your group, melting the stress away and replacing it with newfound energy and exciting ideas for helping your children.

Some Positive Ideas
So, now you have learned how to be a positive advocate. What next? Why, taking action, of course.

Advocating for Mentally Ill Children

- Read books on the subject of your child's illness. Understanding an illness makes it less frightening and gives you more knowledge.
- Join a support or advocacy group that supports uses positive methods to advocate.
- Write letters to those who can help in support of increasing the insurance companies' responsibility to the mentally ill.
- Let politicians know your child's story and how the mental healthcare system affects your child and family. Tell them ways that you think they can help improve the system. Keep your letter polite and positive. Or conversely, write letters to politicians that support the mental healthcare system and tell them how much you appreciate all they are doing. Thank them!
- Volunteer time and aid to your local mental health center. Volunteering to help others who have mental health problems will increase your understanding of mental illness and you may aid in finding help for others.
- If you think your child's mental healthcare professional is doing a great job of helping your child, tell the person so! It is a difficult and oftentimes thankless field of endeavor. Professionals need support from families.

Important Ways To Help Your Mentally Ill Child

- Get your child an appointment with a qualified mental health professional to get his or her problem diagnosed and treated.
- Be consistent with the treatment plan.
- Be honest and open with your child about his or her illness and treatment. Communication and love are very important parts of the healing process. Answer any questions that your child may have about mental illness.
- Remember to have fun together. You child is still a child, illness or not. Don't let mental illness paralyze your ability to enjoy each other.

Things You Can Do To Help You!

- Parents often tend to put themselves on the back burner when their child is ill. You are human and you have needs, too. Be kind to and pamper yourself once in a while. This will help to keep you from burning out.
- Rest when you need to. Having a mentally ill child can really drain you both mentally and physically. Take the time to rest and recharge yourself. Leave the child with a qualified sitter and go out with your spouse. You still need time to connect with each other as adults.
- Treat yourself to something you enjoy every now and then. Don't let life become so infused with your child's problems that you no longer enjoy anything.
- Praise yourself for the good job you are doing. It is difficult having a mentally ill child in the family. You deserve to be proud of yourself for all the hard work you are putting into helping that child.
- Write down three things each day that you are thankful for. This will help you put life into perspective and give you a reason to smile in a difficult time.

– c h a p t e r   s e v e n t e e n –

The Positive Way of Life

Now that you've learned the secrets of positive advocacy, you see that it's just old-fashioned kindness and respect for the fellow human beings who are trying to help your mentally ill child. One of the greatest things about positive advocacy is its influence on our children. When our children see us treating others with kindness, gratitude and respect, they tend to mimic our example.

I will always remember the day I discovered that positive advocacy had rubbed off on my daughter, Jessica. She had bought something that broke almost immediately. Jessica had worked hard to save up for this item and its breaking was a big disappointment to her. Instead of getting upset, she asked me to help her write the company a letter using the methods of positive advocacy. My heart was swelling with pride as she and I sat down at my computer to compose the letter. To make a long story short, within two weeks Jessica had a letter from the company and a gift certificate for a replacement.

I recently had a very exciting experience because of my positive advocacy methods. Our home state, North Carolina, has received a lot of bad publicity in a regional newspaper because of some problems within the mental health system. The goal of the articles seemed to be to highly promote strong-arm advocacy methods: Complain about and criticize the system until somebody listens and does something. While the writer of this series certainly had her heart in the right place, her articles portrayed the state's mental healthcare system as incompetent and uncaring, which is very far removed from the truth. Everyone that I have met in the local mental healthcare system has been kind, empathetic and totally dedicated to helping Tommy. The newspaper articles were destroying morale in mental healthcare professionals all over the state. Knowing that this negative publicity was casting these amazing people in a bad light, I couldn't just stand back and not take some kind of positive action!

Sitting down at my trusty computer, I did something I never, ever, imagined I might do. I wrote a letter to the governor of my state. In my letter, I explained how my stepson and our family had our lives essentially saved because of the wonderful people at my local mental health agency. I let him know that this agency was a good role model for the state and that just because there were problems with the system did not mean that everything was rotten. I also included a paper that I had written for the people who work hard every day at local mental health facilities. It was titled, "Have You Thanked Your Local Mental Healthcare Worker Today?" and appears in an earlier chapter of this book. This was a paper I had written and sent to my local mental healthcare agency to tell them how much I appreciated their help.

I felt good pouring my heart out about how these wonderful people had stepped into my life and helped my severely mentally ill stepson. It was important to me that these people be recognized for their contribution to the mentally ill. A few weeks later, I got a call from a woman who works in the state Department of Social Services who said that my paper had touched her. I was just thrilled that someone knew how I felt about the wonderful mental healthcare professionals who have helped us. Not long after, I got a letter from the governor, thanking me for telling him what was right about the mental healthcare system in our state. He, too, had been affected by the bad publicity and the overall shadow it had cast on a system that is pretty good overall. His letter was one of the biggest thrills of my life. The highest official in our state government had heard my tiny little voice, all because I focused on the positive when I wrote to him. Positive letters seem to have a profound way of inspiring people to want to help, especially when it comes to helping children in need. Try it yourself. Write a positive letter to a state official and I will bet that the response will be as good as the one I got.

Positive advocacy has essentially been a part of my life since childhood. I learned that kindness is the very best way to treat everyone we come in contact with. We all have choices to make when it comes to advocating for the children that we love and I have chosen to use kindness, respect for others and gratitude to advocate for my mentally ill stepson. Positive advocacy has allowed me to find the help my stepsons desperately needed and also allowed me to feel good about myself when advocating for Tommy. Positive advocacy significantly decreased my family's stress level, allowing us to regain a feeling of being in control of the situation that so often seemed chaotic and frightening. Positive advocacy has effectively changed our lives for the better. You have the power to use positive advocacy to change your life, too!

After six years as a positive advocate, I am still amazed at the results it can accomplish. Positive advocacy is simple and extremely powerful. It can be used in almost every aspect of our daily lives, not just when we are advocating for our mentally ill children. You can use it anywhere and in just about any situation. Positive advocacy will benefit your mentally ill child and your life as well. Other people who help your child will feel good when you treat them in a kind, grateful and respectful manner. You will feel good about yourself when you advocate positively. Everyone wins.

Positive Advocacy—Pass It On!

– epilogue –

Tommy has been hospitalized for over three years, yet our fear of him and for him still lingers. Things have changed in the world around him, but not much seems to have changed in the private hell in which he resides. No medication or therapy seems to break into the bubble that surrounds him like an impenetrable shell. He remains psychotic and disoriented most of the time. Occasionally, a bright moment will shine through, but not often enough for anyone to trust that the anger dwelling within him is fading. It has become clear that he is going to need a lifetime of care. He is damaged and we can no longer live on the crumbs of hope that he will ever be what society calls "normal."

Accepting that I couldn't help Tommy was my biggest personal hurdle to overcome. When he left, I felt as if I had failed. I had always thought that if you loved someone hard enough their wounded hearts could be healed. It was hard to face the fact that I couldn't just love Tommy and make all his trauma disappear. However, after three years of professional help—around the clock—Tommy was still trapped inside his own world, a private hell from which no one can seem to free him. It was only recently that I was I able to free myself from the personal feelings of failure that burdened my own heart. I know now I did the best I could. That's all I could have done.

Mark's pain still runs very deep, though he tries hard to shield everyone from it. This was the baby who used to love to swim with Mark and his father. This was the child he rocked in his arms to sleep. Tommy was his firstborn son—Mark's hopes for the future—the first to carry on the Henry name. Seeing all those dreams squashed has left him very saddened.

The children in the house have grown so much. Nevertheless, the older three bear the scars of Tommy's presence here very deeply. Having him here changed us all. They are too young to understand that Mark did what he thought best for his son. Mark's love for his children was unconditional, just like his love for Jeff, Kyle and Jessica.

Mark and I and the children took our very first family vacation about a year after Tommy was hospitalized. We all had a wonderful time, but we returned home to read the headlines in the newspaper that the *Willie M.* entitlement was being taken away. Unbeknownst to us, a judge had ruled several months before that the state was doing such a good job with the program that it no longer needed to be court mandated. I guess the judge thought that he could trust the state to continue the precedent that had been set and was working miraculously for children in need of care. His heart must have broken that same morning.

With the swiftness of another judge's gavel falling, the state began to dissolve a program to parents like Mark and me was tantamount to a miracle. I sprang into action to try and save the program, but it was too late. The state had made up its mind to "restructure" the mental healthcare system for the entire state. Mark and I had the security that Tommy would be entitled to care taken away from us, throwing us into a tailspin of day-to-day anxiety and fear. Mental healthcare workers all over the state were suddenly in fear for their jobs. Nobody won that fateful day the state decided it knew best. I wondered if the authorities had even talked to anyone with a mentally ill child. How could our lawmakers sleep at night if they had any real understanding of what families like mine went through? Were they to walk even one day in our shoes, they would have been increasing the very programs they were seeking to cut.

Very soon, Tommy's original hospital closed down and he was transferred to another. A few months later, that one closed as well. After that there were no hospitals to treat children who sexually offend (under the age of twelve) left in our state. Luckily, Patty, Tommy's case manager, came through. She suggested we try a group home that was managed by a man whom she trusted.

Tommy was transferred to the group home. A wonderful man named Henry manages it. He has an attitude of compassion, tempered with an ability to handle kids like Tommy. When I met him I saw Henry wasn't big and burly as I had expected; he was an average sized man with determined will that showed through as he spoke. Henry had come from a large family and had his own share of rough times growing up. This wonderful man had devoted himself to helping children like Tommy and he doesn't give up on any child—no matter how violently he may behave. Most of all, Henry really cares. He is another angel who has come into our lives. We are very lucky.

The state panicked this year and began cutting the mental health budget, blaming the economy. Things remain unstable and uncertain, though I know that the people who are taking care of Tommy realize just how seriously ill he is. I've written articles for legislative magazines, as well as letters to legislators on behalf of seriously mentally ill children. I have learned that there are some out there who fight tirelessly for these children and adults who really need help. Unfortunately there are others out there who only see dollars and have no conscience when it comes to children and adults with severe mental illness. God bless those who truly care; may the prayers of families like my own strengthen them.

Coping with the pressure of the changes to the system severely stresses the mental healthcare workers who care deeply about the jobs they do. Some have given up and gone on to other ventures, others have remained strong and continue to deliver the excellent services to the mentally ill that they feel an inner calling to give. Mark and I pray for the economy to recover and for these wonderful people to again feel job security and peace so that they can go on helping our children.

I think that the biggest problem in reaching the legislature's heart is the fact that so few parents of mentally ill people come forward to tell them of the horrifying experiences they have been through. Why don't more come forward? Stigma. I hope that by writing this book, families who suffer because of severely mentally ill children will understand that they are not alone, that they can come forward to advocate for their children and know that there is no shame in having a child or relative with mental illness.

Tommy was recently suspended from his school for an entire week for hosing down the boy's bathroom with urine. Tommy had asked to use the restroom. The substitute teacher checked the bathroom and found it clean. Tommy went in and used it. When she went back in to check after him, it was covered in his urine. They also found him dancing naked in his room at the group home. He had no explanation as to why. He now claims to hear the voice of a friend named "Bubba." He often quotes what Bubba tells him.

Any change in routine still continues to send Tommy into a tantrum. The group home maintains a rigid schedule for him so that he won't explode. Most kids go through their program for sexual offenders just once. It has been recommended that Tommy continue to go through it indefinitely. He can parrot the things they teach him, but he just doesn't seem to get it. Tommy is referred to as an "opportunist," one who isn't likely to do anything while he's being watched, but who will act out if left unsupervised.

Mark visits Tommy once a month. The pain that Mark experiences when he sees his son is heartbreaking. For days afterward, Mark is solemn and quiet. He was the hero in saving his boys from harm and yet he feels guilt that Tommy is mentally ill. Mark hurts because he feels so helpless. He will probably always wonder *What if?*

It's been brought to our attention that both Tommy and Bobby probably suffer from the effects of their biological mother's drinking during pregnancy. Tommy has been diagnosed with Fetal Alcohol Effects (FAE).

As for Tommy and Bobby's natural mother, when her three daughters told her they were molested by Rod, she filed for divorce. Gayle had quite a fight in divorce court to save her three daughters from being taken away from her. Alice did what she could to help, because she's a woman of honor and her three granddaughters' welfare came above all else. I was so proud of her for that. All the judge did was require Rod to sign a paper admitting guilt, attend a sex-offender's class and order him to stay away from children forever. Gayle is trying hard to get her life back together.

Alice and Will have renewed their relationship with their grand-daughters and are close to Mark, the kids and me. We are still best friends, bonded forever by tragedy and united forever by love. They are part of my family and I truly cherish them.

We lost Mark's mother on February 6, 2001. In her memory, we planted bright, colorful flowers, just like Perry always loved. In the middle of the garden stands a concrete angel statue, to always remind us of her presence. We placed two stepping-stones on each side of the angel: one says "Mom's Garden," and the other says, "Hope."

Although Bobby is still challenged, he can now accept love and love in return. I just have to remind myself that I did the best I could—just like every other parent. It will always hurt that I couldn't break through the wall around Tommy's heart, but I have Bobby to remind me that, sometimes, things can be made better with love, patience and time. Bobby withstood torturous abuse and yet still has the capacity to love. The frail little boy I took into my arms that cold February night is a blessing and every day he wakes up smiling over the simplest and smallest things. He looks forward to his long bus ride to school. He loves his teacher. He is happy. What greater gift could we ask for?

My talented son Jeffrey has become a serious artist. Kyle is doing well in college and has learned to play the acoustic guitar. Jessica is growing up to be a lovely young woman .

Tommy remains a danger to himself and others and we are now discussing adult care for him when that time comes. My prayer is that Tommy is never allowed the chance to hurt anyone. I fear that if he is not constantly watched every minute of the day, he will maim or kill someone. I know that rage still lives within him.

Most people don't expect a stepmother to care, much less try so hard to help such a sick and disturbed child for six years. I did what I could because I loved the children. However, Tommy's problems are just too deep and complicated. It took me a long time not to consider myself a failure. I always believed that love could save him, but I was wrong. Sometimes, you just have to realize that you did the very best you could and you must accept reality.

Above all else, if you see signs of emotional disturbance in your child, don't ignore them, find help! Even if getting help sometimes seems frustrating, never ever give up! Your life, the child's life and the life of the family you love may depend on it.

If you are raising a child like Tommy, please know that there is help. Sometimes it may seem like there isn't any, but beg and plead and advocate hard if you have to, and just keep trying. You may be stretched to your emotional limits, but don't give up.

My goal in life now is to reach out to others going through similar circumstances with mentally ill children and let you know you are not alone and should not despair. Through experience, bitter and hard but rewarding, I have walked your difficult path. With the counsel of Dr. Vincent Pastore, I want to share with you what I have seen and learned—how to best advocate for your mentally ill child and find the aid he or she needs.

– appendix –

Mental Health Resources

Alliance for the Mentally Ill/Friends and Advocates of the Mentally Ill
432 Park Avenue South, Suite 710,
New York, NY 10016
Phone: (212) 684-3365
Fax: (212) 684-3364
Helpline: (212) 684-3264
website: http://www.nami-nyc-metro.org/
email: helpline@naminyc.org

American Schizophrenia Association
(800) 847-3802 (patient advocacy)

DBSA- Depression and Bipolar Support Alliance
730 N. Franklin Street, Suite 501,
Chicago, Illinois 60610
Toll-Free: (800) 826-3632 ext. 164
Office: (312) 642-0049
Fax: (312) 642-7243
website: http://www.dbsalliance.org/

Get Mental Help, Inc.
19206 65th Place NE
Kenmore, WA 98028
(425) 402-6934
website: http://www.mental-health-matters.com
email: info@mental-health-matters.com

Manic-Depressive Illness in Teens
http://www.aacap.org/publications/factsfam/bipolar.htm

National Alliance for the Mentally Ill
Colonial Place Three
2107 Wilson Blvd., Suite 300
Arlington, VA 22201
Main; (703) 523-7600
Fax: (703) 524-9094
website: http://www.nami.org/
email: info@nami.org

National Alliance for Research on Schizophrenia and Depression
60 Cutter Mill Rd, Suite 404
Great Neck, NY 11021
Phone: (800) 829-8289
Fax: (516) 487-6930
website: http://www.narsad.org/
email: info@narsad.org

National Depressive & Manic-Depressive Association
730 North Franklin St. #501
Chicago, IL 60610
Phone: (312) 642-0049
Toll-free: (800) 826-3632 (patient advocacy)
website: http://www.ndmda.org
email: arobinson@ndmda.org

National Foundation for Depressive Illness
P.O. Box 2257
New York, NY 10116
(800) 248-4344 (patient advocacy)

National Mental Health Services Knowledge Exchange Network
P.O. Box 42557
Washington, DC 20015
Toll-Free: (800) 789-2647
Fax: (301) 984-8796
website: http://www.mentalhealth.org
email: ken@mentalhealth.org

Advocacy Groups and Political Contacts

Advocacy Institute
1629 K. St., NW, Suite 200
Washington, DC 20006
Phone: (202) 777-7575
Fax: (202) 777-7577
website: http://www.advocacy.org
email: info@advocacy.org

Bazelon Center for Mental Health Law
1101 15th St. NW #1212
Washington, DC 20005
Phone: (202) 467-5730
Fax: (202) 223-0409
website: http://www.bazelon.org
email: webmaster@bazelon.org

The Federation of Families for Children's Mental Health
1101 King Street, Suite 420
Alexandria, Virginia 22314
Phone: (703) 684-7710
Fax: (703) 836-1040
website: http://www.ffcmh.org (patient advocacy)
email: ffcmh@ffcmh.org

The United States House of Representatives Mailing Address:
The Honorable (name of representative)
U.S. House of Representatives
Washington, DC 20515

The United States Senate Mailing Address:
The Honorable (name of senator)
United States Senate
Washington, DC 20510

President of the United States
The White House
1600 Pennsylvania Avenue
Washington, DC 20500